PRESSURE COOKER

Also by Don Biggs

Breaking Out
Real Money
The Loving Arrangement
Survival Afloat

PRESSURE COOKER

Don Biggs

W · W · Norton & Company
New York

Copyright © 1979 by Don Biggs
Published simultaneously in Canada by George J. McLeod Limited,
Toronto. Printed in the United States of America.
All Rights Reserved

Library of Congress Cataloging in Publication Data
Biggs, Don.
    Pressurecooker.
        1. Air traffic control—United States.
I. Title.
TL725.3.T7B53 1978 387.7′4′042 78–13354
ISBN 0-393–08815–4
1 2 3 4 5 6 7 8 9 0

Dedicated to the air traffic controllers of the Federal Aviation Administration. It's their book.

Contents

8 **Contents**

Acknowledgments

I CAN never fully express my appreciation to the numerous air traffic controllers and their families who spent many hours with me in candid conversation, and who often took me into their homes for varying lengths of time to experience their lives with them.

During my months of research and interviews I was also welcomed into airport control towers, approach and departure control facilities, and en route air traffic control centers with a warmth and openness I shall never forget.

My special thanks also to James Dow, Acting Administrator of the Federal Aviation Administration at the time I began this book, for the FAA's total cooperation.

I am also indebted to John F. Leyden, President of the Professional Air Traffic Controllers Organization (PATCO) and to Darrell Reazin, PATCO's western regional Vice-President, for their continuing assistance.

To these, then, and to many others who could not be named, my special thanks:

Don Alford, Frank Arcidiacono, Don Bailor, Jack Barker, Charles Bell, E. Elliott Benezra, M.D., Merton Berger, M.D., Gerald Bogan, Bill Boyle, Walt Brewer, Nyda Brown, M.D., Bob Buckhorn, Russ Carter, Mike Cherioli, Sidney Cobb, M.D., Ty Cobb, Eric Cohane, Lonnie Conrad, Julie Coryn, Gary Crosby, Sebastian Dangerfield, Ph.D., Don Davis, Jack Dennend, Dave Des Armier, Al Dilger, Judy Dillman, Richard Dillman, Brad Dunbar, Dave Eggers, Steve Eilkins, Jacque Feister, Robert Feister, Gerald Feltman, Joe Fowler, Jack Francis.

Joe Gibbs, Dave Gourley, John Graffius, Ben Sanborn Graham,

10   **Acknowledgments**

Ph.D., Harry Grove, Ray Harding, Peg Harrison, Gabe Harth, Jerry Helvey, Robert Henshaw, M.D., Tim Hetzler, Pete Hobinger, James Holweger, Don Hoseipian, Bob Huber, Austin Hyde, Doug Jernigan, Arthur Kohler, Gene Kropf, Kurt Krumes, Capt. Ray Lahr, Vinnie Lampton, Bill Laningham, Connie Laningham, John G. Leyden, Jim Lindsey.

Capt. Don McBain, Dallas McClemons, Ralph Moore, Richard Morrison, Roger Myers, Barbara Neuwirth, Mary O'Brien, Capt. Francis Pipes, Al Plumridge, Bill Porter, Ed Reed, Robert Rose, M.D., George Rogers, Foster Rupert, Jim Ruse, Roseann Ruse, Jack Ryan, Steve Sacca, James Senecal, Dennis Shattuck, Elizabeth Shattuck, Mark Sheffield, Dave Siegel, Travis Smith, Howard Stacey, Bob Starkey, James Strother, Stan Stuka, Philip Swatek, Jim Tittle, Richard Troup, Gerald Tuso, Diane Tyler, Michael Wandrick, Ronald Washington, Bill White, Hank Whitney, Jim Wilhelm, Joe Witta, Ancil Young, Robert Young.

Finally, my thanks to "Pete" Kerr for research assistance and preparation of the final manuscript.

Introduction

THIS BOOK is the story of air traffic controllers at work—a job which routinely makes them individually responsible for more lives than the practitioners of any other occupation in the United States.

The controllers whose work I followed each day for nearly six months are the men and women who "man" the airport control tower and radar room at Los Angeles International Airport, and who sit before the radars of the Los Angeles Air Route Traffic Control Center at Palmdale, California, some sixty miles northeast of Los Angeles. With more than 1,200 landings and takeoffs every twenty-four hours, Los Angeles International (LAX) is the world's third busiest airline terminal, outranked only by Chicago O'Hare and Atlanta International.

But one of the things which makes LAX unique, and perhaps more demanding on controllers than either O'Hare or Atlanta, is that within forty miles of its boundaries are located four of the seven busiest airports in the world—each busier even than Kennedy, LaGuardia, Newark, Washington National, San Francisco, or Dallas–Ft. Worth. While LAX serves mostly airlines, the Los Angeles basin's other airports handle traffic consisting of not only airliners, but also the general aviation fleet of corporate jets and multi- and single-engine planes which move more than 50 percent of the people who fly from one city to another every year. At any given moment, more than one-fourth of the air traffic aloft over the United States is above the 40- by 100-mile Los Angeles basin, denying LAX's controllers the luxury of holding-patterns often used at other cities to stack airliners during arrival rushes and when instrument approaches must be flown.

Like controllers at major airports everywhere, those at Los Angeles have no control over the rate of their work. Whatever comes their way must be dealt with instantly, and every minute they live with the anxiety of knowing the consequences of an error. Once a controller is working

11

a busy position, only he "has the picture" and no one else can help.

I began the Los Angeles phase of my research only after receiving the Federal Aviation Administration's permission for frequent visits to its facilities in the area. I was never denied a single request by the FAA officials I met and dealt with. Though they probably had a natural concern about the ultimate consequences of any journalist having free access to possibly embarassing information, no door was ever closed to me and no official ever turned aside a question with a terse "no comment."

No conditions were laid down for me to follow, no promises were exacted, and no releases were placed before me to sign. But there were certain conditions I imposed upon myself:

In the event of a serious accident to which I happened to be a witness, or about which I obtained confidential information by virtue of my position, I would write nothing beyond that which was available to the public; at no time would I report anything I saw to the FAA regional management, the FAA headquarters in Washington, or the press; and I would not knowingly write anything which would endanger any controller's career, his family relationships, or his relationships with other controllers.

Generally, I "worked" a regular shift at each of the major facilities I visited. I talked with controllers on and off the job and spoke with their families. I was invited to their homes and was asked along on weekend trips to the beach and to bars at the end of a day's work.

Almost everywhere I employed a battery-powered casette recorder and transcribed the tapes before beginning to write. Quotes included on the pages of this book are as accurate as I could make them. I have not eliminated any profanity, since it is an important part of controllers' work talk. Since it was important to name the facilities I visited, the names of controllers I interviewed at length have been changed to preserve their privacy. Other controllers with a personal knowledge of events will recognize those I have written about.

If I was impressed with any one thing, it was the controllers' absolute dedication to their work. The personal price they pay is too great for their commitment to be otherwise.

Though it was never discussed, but perhaps should have been, I could not help but sense the respect and affection which controllers working together felt for each other. The responsibilities they share in an occupation the world knows almost nothing about seemed to create a quality of emotional contact seldom achieved among even the closest of families.

Controllers often mentioned the need they felt to avoid any appearance of incompetence or inadequacy, but none ever mentioned the care they took to never make a remark which raised doubts about another controller's competence. Their thoughtfulness even extended to almost never embarassing a pilot in any way on the radio. When a controller was having a bad day or serious family problems he was, without a word and for as long as necessary, "carried" until he was on his emotional and intellectual feet again.

"When you're carrying a guy," one controller explained, "you tell the assistant chief, 'Hey, let me stay here a little while longer,' because when you stay in the hot spot a while longer, the other guy's going to stay in the easy spot a while longer. But you never say, 'Let him stay there a little bit longer,' because then you'd be getting to his ego. You carry each other, but nobody says anything because we've all been there."

On the following pages, I have attempted to impose myself as little as possible upon the controllers' words. It was occasionally necessary, so that the reader would be able to understand the controllers' experiences, for me to explain some aspects of air traffic control. This I have tried to do as succinctly as possible.

I have also included, in two or three places, several pages of the actual, rapid-fire radio "traffic" which passes between controllers and pilots during a busy period. Though there may be a temptation to scan these passages to "get on with the book," to do so would be to miss an opportunity to appreciate the necessarily faultless handling of the numbers involved: speeds, headings, altitudes, distances, flight numbers, runways, wind directions, wind velocities, and visibilities—all of which must be stated and understood with perfection.

I have described a number of accidents which took place at other airports, not in any effort to add sensationalism, but to give the reader a better basis to comprehend the controller's fear of making even the smallest mistake.

Finally, I have included some of the "sea stories" of early air traffic control, plus recommendations for improving an air traffic system which was described in a study prepared by a group of airline pilots in 1976 as, "reaching a point of critical mass. . . ."

PRESSURE COOKER

1 The Spider Web That Grew Too Slowly

It was all moving so fast in those days [from 1935 to 1955] that none of us could keep up. We went from the Ford Tri-Motor to four-engine, pressurized airliners, from practically no navigational aids at all to four-course radio range stations to VORs. We went from no en route centers at all to more than we have today [in 1976]. It seemed like you went home, and every time you came back on duty there was a new radio or a new teletype or some new procedure you had to learn. Every day it was a whole new ballgame—and still it wasn't fast enough.

—Retired Air Traffic Controller

LOS ANGELES International Airport, with its four parallel runways, its 495,000 yearly landings and takeoffs, and its twenty-four-hour-a-day, seven-days-a-week control tower and radar approach and departure control, is outranked in airline operations by only Chicago O'Hare and Atlanta International. There are nineteen additional high density terminal control areas which encompass the airspace of other major airports in the United States.

Of the nation's 6,000 airports, about 500 are tower-controlled. Although radar approach and departure facilities serve about 160 of the 500 towers, only about 65 of these have the latest radar which shows a plane's flight number, altitude, and ground speed. At the other radar facilities, controllers have to remember which plane is which, and how high each is flying.

Important as they are, airports with control towers and radar would be like scattered links of a chain without air route traffic control centers (also called en route centers) to tie them together. Everything that Los Angeles International, Chicago O'Hare, and JFK have to offer would be useless if there were no way of preventing mid-air collisions between planes flying from one city to another. It is the twenty-one air route traffic control centers around the United States which monitor air routes with radar to keep aircraft apart in instrument weather and at jet altitudes where planes fly too fast for the pilots to see each other in time to avoid collision.

If it could be made visible and seen from satellite altitude, the United States airway system nearest earthly resemblance might be a vast, interconnected spider web, with the biggest spiders living in transportation hubs like Los Angeles, Dallas, Chicago, Washington, New York, Miami, Atlanta, Boston, and San Francisco. The airways converge there, just as the strands of a spider's web converge at its lair.

Long ago, as pilots measure time, airways were marked by symbols on the ground and by flashing beacons followed, anxiously, at night. Today, airways are still numbered, but on charts. Just as U.S. 40 reaches from the Atlantic to the Pacific, so does airway J-64 and scores of others. And just as U.S. 1 stretches from Maine to Miami, so does airway J-79. The time has long since passed when pilots looked out the window to check progress along their course. Navigation, even on bright, sunny days, is by radio, and, if you keep the needles of your navigational instruments where they're supposed to be, you will arrive, precisely, where you want to go. Pilots still make note of crossing the Mississippi or the Grand Canyon, passing the southern tip of Lake Michigan, or flying over Dallas; but they do it with the confidence of an old-time railroad conductor who could look at his watch as his train pulled through a town and know perfectly well which town it was because he was always exactly on time.

Everyone aloft flies the same system: airliners and military planes, corporate jets, light twins owned by companies in towns not served by airlines, and single-engine planes flown by salesmen covering their territories by air instead of by road. The airway system, invisible as it is, is far from nebulous. All aircraft above 18,000 feet, where even small planes fly today, follow exact flight plans confirmed by computer, and each pilot's course is determined ahead of time, from airway to airway, at assigned altitudes. Airborne equipment, constantly "talking" with air route center computers, combines with ground-based computers to display each plane's number, altitude, and groundspeed in a little block of numbers which follows each plane's blip as it moves along the air traffic controller's radar display. Radio communications, computer-generated radar displays, and flight plans strictly adhered to serve to keep the 16,000 planes which are aloft over the United States at any given moment from conflicting with each other.

There were only 3,000 miles of marked airways in the entire United States (compared with more than 125,000 miles of airways today) when Lindbergh took off from Los Angeles on the first west to east transcontinental airline flight. If he'd been less of a navigator, he might not have found Clovis, New Mexico, at the end of his Ford Tri-Motor's first day of historic flight. Almost until the day of Lindbergh's 1929-transcontinental flight, airways existed in name only. The Wright Brothers airway followed the southern route across the United States from San Diego to Washington. The Wilson airway stretched between New York and San Francisco. Shorter routes, like railroads or stagecoach lines, often took the names of cities they served. Pilots flying cross-country in 1922 were advised that airways were eighty miles wide (compared with ten today), because forty miles was judged to be the distance a pilot flying at 5,000 feet on a clear day could see to either side of his course. Informal rules called for keeping to the right, and avoiding the no-man's-land of the airway centerline to prevent mid-air collisions.

But air-ground radio existed when Lindbergh flew to Clovis in 1929, and by the mid-thirties en route radio beacons began to link airports so that planes could fly from one city to another without reference to the ground. The directional beacons broadcast by early navigational stations were more or less in the shape of a cross, with each beacon's four arms aligned as nearly as possible along airways from airport to airport. In two quadrants of the cross, say between twelve o'clock and three o'clock and between six o'clock and nine o'clock, only morse code for the letter "A" (•–) could be heard. In the other two quadrants, only the letter "N" (–•) could be heard. But, along the four lines where the quadrants were tangent, dot-dash of the "A" and dash-dot of the "N" merged to create a continuous tone. As long as a pilot heard the continuous tone in his earphones he was on course. If the sound of the "A" or the "N" began to predominate, he knew he was drifting off the airway and he turned his plane a few degrees "into" his route until he heard the unbroken tone again. But the four-course navigational signals were highly subject to static during storms—just when they were needed most—and listening to them prevented pilots from communicating with the ground while following a beam.

What pilots wanted was a form of radio navigation which wasn't affected by weather, which presented its information visually, and which provided more than the four courses presently broadcast by each station. But such a system wasn't to become available for twenty years. In the meantime, airline service provided by the navigation system with which pilots were struggling was surprisingly "modern." By 1938, hundreds of four-course radio range stations formed a framework for more than 63,000 miles of all-weather airways; and, using a low-powered, single-beam modification of the four-course, en route beacons, pilots were making safe "blind" landings out of clouds whose base was as low as 400 feet above the surface—in visibility of barely a mile.

The twin-engine DC-3, certified in 1936, quickly eclipsed

the Ford Tri-Motor and every other plane flying the skies. It was a magnificent machine. With a cruising speed of 180 miles an hour, the DC-3 offered a soundproof, heated cabin with comfortable reclining seats, in-flight meals, individual reading lights, and, on overnight coast-to-coast flights, sleeping berths as luxurious as those on any Pullman car. By the late thirties, DC-3s were carrying 90 percent of all airline traffic and flying was beginning to be thought of by many regular passengers as just one more safe, reliable means of travel. In 1940, thanks largely to the DC-3, the airlines scored their first full year of operations without a single passenger or crew fatality.

In 1935, the first air route traffic control center was established at Newark airport to keep airline pilots in the vicinity advised of the whereabouts of other planes in the area. In 1936, en route centers were commissioned at Chicago, Detroit, Pittsburgh, and Cleveland. The Los Angeles, Washington, and Oakland centers were commissioned in 1938, and en route centers at St. Louis, Salt Lake City, Ft. Worth, and Atlanta opened the following year. At first, centers provided traffic separation using time and altitude assignments. The system required frequent position reports by pilots and consumed large amounts of airspace, since extended portions of airways had to be reserved for every plane. Already, aviation people were beginning to talk of crowded skies.

Air traffic controllers wrote each flight's number, flight plan route, and altitude on slips of paper which they attached to plastic markers and pushed along a plotting board each time a pilot radioed-in to report his position. A sudden sneeze could blow away the entire sky. The en route system remained pretty much the same during, and for several years after, World War II. Radar was first tested for air traffic control in 1935, but it wasn't until 1946 that the first radar-equipped control tower went into operation at Indianapolis. Radar was ideal for providing aircraft separation in crowded terminal areas and, within a few years, radar approach and departure control was available at major airports.

Five years after the first terminal area radar went into service, pilots finally got the radio navigation system they wanted. Phased into use during the early fifties, the new stations, called VORs (Visual Omnidirectional Range), were, like FM radio, free of static interference. They presented their information visually, allowing pilots to use their communications radios while following a course. Finally, the new stations broadcast 360 separate "beams," one for each point of the compass, so that many airways could benefit from each station. All a pilot had to do was tune to the station and select the course he wanted to follow. By keeping a vertical needle in the center of a dial he remained on course. The system was reliable, static-free, and easy to use. Its only disadvantage, and one pilots were willing to live with, was its relatively short range. VOR signals were (and still are) line-of-sight, which meant that low-flying planes had to be fairly close to a station to receive its signal. By the mid-fifties, the old four-course range stations were being phased out: there were 65,000 miles of VOR airways, compared with 50,000 miles of four-course airways.

Although radar approach and departure traffic separation was being provided at major airports, en route traffic separation was still based on altitude assignments and pilot position reports. Combined civil-military use of Air Force long-range defense radar had been suggested for en route traffic control in 1947, but implementation remained snagged in a tangle of bureaucratic red tape. Finally, in 1956, the Civil Aeronautics Administration (forerunner of the FAA) and the Air Force announced a joint study on the use of military radar for civil en route traffic control. Moreover, during the 1950s, the skies became increasingly populated with the second generation of modern airliners, four-engine Super-Constellations and DC-7s, flying higher and faster than anything the system had handled before.

It soon became obvious to controllers that the system's slow reaction time, resulting from intermittent, relayed position reports as planes passed over widely-spaced fixes, was being out-paced by the performance of newer aircraft. But it took a major air disaster to give controllers the tools they needed to cope with the demands they faced.

2   Mid–Air at 10:31

No greater evil could befall aviation than a fatal collision between two large transports.

—Jerome Lederer, Director
Flight Safety Foundation
February, 1956

THERE WAS nothing unusual about the local controller's view from Los Angeles tower on the morning of June 30, 1956. He'd just departed an American Airlines DC-7 for Dallas, handed the flight off to departure control, and was watching for a Delta Air Lines DC-6, due any second to descend from the floor of the 700-foot overcast for landing on 25 Right. With Delta out of the way, he'd be able to depart TWA 2, a Lockheed Constellation, nonstop to Kansas City. On the pad behind the Constellation, the crew of a United Airlines DC-7 their plane's four engines and cycled its propellors readying for takeoff. During the few moments he'd have before the next arrival touched down on 25 Right, the controller hoped he'd have enough time to depart both TWA 2 and United 718. TWA 2, he knew, was already half an hour behind schedule because of a maintenance delay.

At exactly 9:00 A.M., as the Delta arrival turned from the runway toward the terminal, the controller cleared TWA 2 for takeoff. Almost immediately, he told the DC-7, "Taxi into position and hold two five Right; be prepared for immediate takeoff." At 9:04, three minutes after TWA 2's wheels left the runway, United 718 was cleared for takeoff and disappeared into the overcast en route to Chicago.

Soon after departing LAX, the pilot of TWA 2 requested a change from his original flight plan and was turned right to a reading of 31 degrees along VOR airway 210 toward the Daggett VOR, 137 miles northeast of Los Angeles.

United 718 was turned left along Green airway 5 (in a four-course radio range) on a heading of 78 degrees to Palm Springs.

With both planes flying in unlimited visibility on top of the 2,400-foot overcast which existed in the Los Angeles area, control for the flights was handed off to the Los Angeles Air Route Traffic Control Center for en route monitoring as they proceded eastward.

United 718 was cleared to Palm Springs at 21,000 feet, then, to a heading of 43 degrees for 133 miles, to the Needles VOR. From Needles, it would fly direct to the Painted Desert reporting fix, then direct to Durango, direct to Pueblo, direct to St. Joseph, via VOR airway 116 to Joliet, and via VOR airway 84 to Chicago Midway Airport.

At 9:21, through TWA radio, flight 2 requested a change in flight plan altitude from 19,000 to 21,000 feet. The TWA operator receiving the request called Los Angeles center via land line, "TWA 2 is coming up on Dagget requesting two one thousand feet." Upon receiving the request, the Los Angeles controller contacted the Salt Lake center controller into whose airspace TWA 2 would soon be moving. "TWA 2 is requesting two one thousand," he said. "How does it look? I see you have United 718 crossing at his altitude—in his way at two one thousand."

"Yes," the Salt Lake controller replied, "their courses cross and they're right together."

Just as the Los Angeles controller was advising the TWA radio operator that the center was unable to approve 21,000 feet, the TWA operator interrupted, "Just a minute, I think he wants a thousand on top—yes, a thousand on top if he can get it."

After determining that TWA 2 was at that time at least 1,000 feet on top (of the clouds), Los Angeles center advised, "ATC clears TWA 2 to maintain at least one thousand feet on top. Your traffic is United 718, direct Durango, estimating Needles at 9:57."

The TWA operator relayed the clearance verbatim to flight 2, adding from his own knowledge that United 718 was at 21,000.

Collision avoidance under visual conditions was, and still is, the responsibility of pilots. TWA 2 and the United 718 would soon be operating on "direct" routings, off controlled airways. CAA controllers would therefore expect them to provide their own separation from other aircraft. CAA regulations specified that "no responsibility for separation of aircraft outside controlled airspace is accepted." Although the same rule holds true today, traffic advisories are nearly always available, even to the smallest plane, thanks to long-range radar, transponders, computer-generated data blocks, and instant communication between controllers and planes at almost any location.

But in 1956, without radar, lacking direct communication with aircraft in many areas, and having only intermittent position reports, it was impossible for center controllers to closely monitor the relative positions of TWA 2 and United 718. Any interpretation controllers could make about planes' positions lagged several minutes behind actual conditions because the planes quickly outflew the data. Strips of paper were a poor substitute for the visual traffic situation controllers needed—but didn't have.

At 9:59, missing its estimate by only two minutes, United 718 reported over the Needles VOR at 21,000 feet, estimating Painted Desert at 10:31.

Also at 9:59, TWA 2 reported that it had passed Lake Mohave at 9:55, and estimated Painted Desert at 10:31.

After receiving TWA 2's report, the CAA Las Vegas communicator called Salt Lake center on land line interphone to relay the flight's position and estimate of reaching Painted Desert at 10:31.

At 10:13, the Needles CAA communicator called Salt Lake center to relay United 718's position, its 21,000-foot cruising altitude, and its estimate of also reaching Painted Desert at 10:31.

The same controller received and posted both reports.

As the planes continued eastward, clouds which at first had been scattered along their routes at 15,000 feet intensified and became a solid layer at that altitude with occasional thunderheads towering above 25,000 feet. To remain in visual conditions the pilots flew around, rather than through, the build-ups along their routes.

At 10:31, thirty-six minutes after TWA 2 passed Lake Mohave, and thirty-three minutes after United 718 passed Needles, and possibly as the two planes emerged from opposite sides of a cloud which had prevented the pilots from seeing each other, the left wingtip of the DC-7 sliced into the upper, center fin of the Constellation's three-rudder tail. At the same instant, the propellor of the DC-7's left outboard engine inflicted a series of cuts in the aft baggage compartment of the Constellation. Immediately afterward, the lower surface of the DC-7 struck the upper aft fuselage of the Constellation with disintegrating force, destroying the DC-7's outer wing panel. The collision ripped open the top of the Constellation's fuselage from just forward of the tail to just aft of the main cabin door. The Constellation pitched down and fell in a very steep descent to the ground. The DC-7, minus most of its left wing, and with severe damage to its left horizontal stabilizer, fell in a turning path and impacted the earth in the Grand Canyon 1.3 miles from the wreckage of the Constellation.

At 10:31, the radio communicator at Salt Lake heard, "Salt Lake, United 718 . . . ah . . . we're going in." No transmission was heard from TWA 2. Sixty-four passengers and a crew of six aboard the Constellation, and fifty-three passengers and a crew of five aboard the DC-7 died in the crash.

Eighteen minutes before the collision, at approximately 10:13, the Salt Lake center controller was in possession of the last position reports made by the two planes. He had been informed that both aircraft were operating at 21,000 feet, were on converging courses, and were estimating Painted Desert at the same time. But the two planes were in *uncontrolled* airspace and the controller was busy working other traffic in controlled airspace for which he was directly responsible. Possibly because the positions and altitudes of TWA 2 and United 718 were merely numbers on pieces of paper, their impending collision failed to register in his mind. He advised neither flight of the situation.

In its final report on the accident, the Civil Aeronautics Board stated that "Accurate and worthwhile traffic information requires that the controller be informed of the aircraft involved and have precise and timely information on their relative positions and altitudes." But TWA 2 and United 718 were flying in airspace which was uncontrolled because the CAA lacked the people and equipment to control it.

For years, since the introduction of modern propellor airliners, the nation's antiquated en route traffic control system had made a collision such as the Grand Canyon mid-air almost inevitable. Without radar, and in the face of booming air travel, controllers needed to provide at least ten minutes separation between planes at the same altitude along airways. In distance, that meant 60 miles for a 360 mph prop plane. For jets, due to begin service in 1958, 100 miles would be required. With no increase in the number of flights, the replacement of prop planes with jets would crowd the airways beyond capacity. The collision had been merely a matter of of time.

Within months after the Grand Canyon mid-air, much sooner than bureaucrats and Air Force generals had said it could ever be done, long-range military radars were being phased into service by en route centers to provide traffic separation along United States airways. The following year, in a knee-jerk reaction compared to putting up a stop sign after a child has been run over at the corner, Congress gave the CAA enough money to hire 1,400 additional air traffic controllers. However, *before* the Grand Canyon crash, the CAA had submitted a five-year plan to buy and install sixty-nine long-range radars plus the attendant communications equipment for en route control, and to nearly double the number of VOR's—from 498 to 881; *after* the Grand Canyon disaster, in a rush to adjourn for the summer, the House and Senate cut $23 million from the $69-million first phase of the CAA's five-year airways improvement program.

3 The Superstars

I've got to admit that the main reason I came to LAX was so I could say I played in the big leagues. I think you do it to prove to yourself that you're big-league quality. It's status. There are four or five places like this: O'Hare, Kennedy, Newark, LaGuardia, maybe Atlanta. I don't have to tell anyone how good I am; if I work at LAX they know it.

THE CONTROL tower I looked up to as I stepped outside the airport terminal where I'd retrieved my luggage stood 172 feet tall near Los Angeles International's main entrance. Put into service in 1961, ten years after completion of its basic construction, it was already beginning to look like a period piece compared to the soaring, sculptured concrete of newer towers whose six- and eight-sided tinted glass control "cabs" were set, like many-faceted jewels, upon graceful pedestals.

I knew, from studying the record, that a controller who worked at Los Angeles tower handled as many planes, and would certainly be responsible for many more lives, during a single busy hour as were handled at some airport towers in an entire day. An

FAA official at the very highest level had told me privately that LAX controllers "move more airplanes every day than anyone in Washington ever thought possible. They are," he said, "superstars." The men and women who work at LAX tower, and those who sit at radarscopes in an isolated building across the field, are, in many respects, as separate from the rest of society as seamen who spend their working lives aboard ship, and as distant from the rest of the world as the fraternity of cops who are among us, but, in their own thinking at least, not of us. Controllers' rapid-turnover shift work—two days of 7:00 A.M. to 3:00 P.M., two days of 3:00 P.M. to 11:00 P.M., and one mid-watch of 11:00 P.M. to 7:00 A.M.—makes outside relationships difficult. Controllers' friends are other controllers.

I had long known that air traffic controllers work in two primary areas:

Terminal Control, airport towers and radar approach and departure control; and

En Route Control, shepherding planes from departure point to destination—over any area of the United States—using radar and radio communication to keep planes safely apart.

I was to learn that the job demands of terminal control and en route control are as divergent as the skills required of a cop who works the financial district and one whose beat is the ghetto.

I already knew that controllers' varying responses to the stress of work were as different as they were sometimes dangerous. I had spoken, months before, with a senior controller in an eastern city who supported four children and had no place to go with the skills he felt he was losing. He had applied for transfer to a smaller, less demanding airport, but experienced controllers were hard to come by at the field where he worked and the FAA was reluctant to let him move. In the meantime, while he continued his campaign for transfer, he regularly went to work each day with several fresh oranges in his lunch box—into which he'd injected vodka with a hypodermic needle.

I had interviewed other senior men who'd become impotent when they felt their quick reaction time at the radarscope had begun to slip. And I had met a young, sportscar-driving controller in the south whose daily route to work took him through an alley near the airport so that, without fear of discovery, he could retch up the meal his wife had served before he'd left home.

There was more I hoped to learn before I began spending my days and nights with different control-shifts in Los Angeles International's tower and radar rooms and at the Los Angeles en route center, more than fifty miles away on the far side of the mountains which form the eastern wall of the Los Angeles basin.

One of my sources was a study of Los Angeles air traffic controllers, conducted by a California management consultant as part of his Ph.D. dissertation.[1] Reading his report in my motel room the night of my arrival, I scanned the statements of controllers he had interviewed.

You grow old quick. As you get old you have too many feelings. You see the older guys watch a [radar] target with a relative on it until it's off the scope, not real cautiously, but they just do it.

Some of the older and some of the younger guys haven't got it. We carry them. It's not always by their choice that they're put in easy positions during difficult traffic. A lot of facilities have ten or so that they're carrying. . . . Most of them admit defeat here.

A couple of months ago I'm on Downey [approach control] east, fifteen [airplanes] simultaneously at the same altitude. It was an unbelievable hour. I don't know how I got out of it. It was as fast as I could talk. I was depending upon my experience and earned my salary then, even if it was only once a year. It takes a while to cool down. The coordinator told my supervisor about it and I got a letter of commendation.

I think I seek reassurance; I don't really care about recognition. I like to get it, but I don't press for it.

1. Ben Sanborn Graham, Jr., "Career Mastery: A Study of Growth and Decline of Occupational Identity Among Air Traffic Controllers at Los Angeles International Airport." (Ph.D. diss., University of California 1969). Excerpts reprinted by permission of the author.

The old guys humiliate the trainees. They try to convince us that we're awfully stupid people. I terminated [at Los Angeles] because of the pressure of the older guys, not the pressure of the traffic.

The report went on to observe that "The primary reaction [by trainees] to degrading treatment appears to be abandonment of interest in social relations. . . . Social relationships which are friendly are criticized because they are not serious enough. Social relationships which are unpleasant are criticized because they represent nonlegitimate stress. . . . And, when senior controllers are fading, they find themselves alone . . . Since even the best controllers can expect to perform in the 'majors' for a limited number of years, they have only a short time to show something which will gain them promotion. If they don't show it, or if there are no promotions available when their time runs out, they are expected to decline. When this time comes, they can anticipate little support."

The older guys hiding in the weeds, making good money, but not doing the work, are a worthless drag on the other guys. When the older guys can't do it, they're carried along. There's no place to put them. The older guys should get out.

Even if you're going down the drain, you can't let the other controllers know it, or they'll help you down.

"Air traffic control at Los Angeles," concluded the report, "creates a changing pattern of increasing stress which, after a very few years of acceptance and esteem, leaves a man in his early forties with little feeling of self-worth, and with narrow job skills which are almost impossible to transfer to some other means of employment."

But, perceptive as it was, the study I read had been conducted nearly eight years before, prior to the time when labor-saving, flight-plan-computers became a part of the air traffic system, and before the interface of sophisticated airborn equipment and improved radar had made the job, in theory at least, a lot easier than it had been.

After checking in with the FAA's regional public affairs officer my first morning in Los Angeles, I talked with one of the FAA's top administrators about how and why air traffic control accidents, mid-air collisions, and near mid-airs happen.

"You know," he told me as we sat in his office looking out over nearby industrial buildings partially obscured by the same pollution which often restricts pilots' visibility at LAX, "you examine it every way you can and you still can't figure it out. You have a mid-air, or a near mid-air you're lucky enough to learn about, and you look at the controllers' backgrounds. You find that the errors were committed by the controllers who were well thought of, well-trained, healthy, and at the peak of their power. They weren't unhappy with their lot; they didn't have an accident driving to work; and they had been on duty only a couple of hours. They weren't even very busy; yet, hearing '9,000 feet,' they wrote down '7,000 feet'; or they just didn't see two targets converging.

"All of a sudden you've got people and airplanes falling out of the sky; and you've got a happy, rested, well-trained controller who simply made a cerebral error. "You can tell me he wasn't paying attention. Well, what's attention? How do you *pay* attention? How do you know when you're *not* concentrating?"

It has happened to me. I can't count the times in my life when I'll be reading, get to the bottom of the page, realize I don't know what I've read, and have to go back and read the page again. And on long trips in the past I've driven through a small town, stopped for all the traffic signals, made all the turns, and then not been able for a second or two to remember *anything* about the town.

I know the FAA has repeatedly studied excellent air traffic controllers to determine what makes a good controller good. And, just when they think they have an answer, one of their best controllers is suddenly responsible for a mid-air or near mid-air collision. On a hunch, because air traffic control is often described as a three-dimensional game of chess, the FAA hired a couple of champion chess players and taught them to be controllers. In training, they sorted out the most complicated air traffic situations with unerring logic. On the job, they required half a minute to arrive at decisions which needed to be made in seconds.

Although the FAA isn't convinced that it has discovered the best means of selecting safe controllers, it has, I found out, learned a lot. On one commonly used test designed to measure sixteen personality characteristics, controllers and airline pilots score above average on intelligence to exactly the same degree: 7.5 on a scale of 0 to 10. Controllers score 6 on the 0 to 10 emotional stability scale compared to 7.5 for airline pilots. Controllers are a bit less "happy-go-lucky" than pilots, according to the test, and are not quite so bold and venturesome. Airline pilots score as less tough-minded, less trusting, and less practical than controllers, but only slightly so. Controllers score as somewhat more apprehensive than pilots, but slightly less apprehensive than the general population.

The greatest difference between pilots and controllers is on the relaxed-tense scale, where controllers appear to be considerably more tense than pilots, scoring five on that scale compared to three for pilots.

On the Strong Vocational Interest Test, a widely-used rating scale, controllers score very high on the masculinity scale. They are oriented toward sports, the outdoors, business, and adventuresome activities—away from intellectual and cultural interests. Controllers score very high on the Interest Test's technical supervision scale, which includes the occupations of production manager, army officer, and air force officer. They show the least interest in the occupations of minister, school superintendent, physicist, and mathematician. Controllers tend to enjoy playing poker, working on cars, and engaging in competitive activities more than does the general population. One item which was checked on the Interest Test by an unusually high number of controllers showed that they would have a strong interest in "pursuing bandits in a sheriff's posse."

Finally, outstanding controllers were highly verbal, outgoing, and young: twenty to thirty-two years of age. Few had completed college, many were married, and all, of course, were earning a good income. Ironically, controllers' relatively high pay, $20,000 to $35,000 a year at major airports, may be a negative factor in safety control.

Ability, rather than education, social refinement, or contacts, enables a controller to move ahead. "Where else," asked the FAA administrator I talked to, "can a sharp kid with no college education be making $20,000 a year, four years out of high school? You get a job like that when you're in your early twenties, say you're married with a kid and another one on the way, and you're paying for a house and a car, you're going to hang onto that job even if you realize you haven't got what it takes to be really good. You'll fake a show of confidence—anything to keep that job—and sooner or later you make a mistake."

Interesting as it was, everything I'd learned about controllers since arriving in Los Angeles was theoretical: an eight-year-old, and possibly no longer valid, study; an interview with a concerned administrator; and a perusal of psychological test results which the FAA admitted were far off the mark in determining the kind of man or woman who could be a safe air traffic controller.

The following day I would join a regular shift in Los Angeles International's tower and begin to learn about controllers at work.

4   LAX, 5:00 P.M.

The job is very demanding. Our health changes, we age three times as fast as we should. It takes you four or four and a half hours to relax after the job. The body gets off cycle with the rotating shifts. Sleep is not really relaxed; it's exhausting.

THE EVENING rush hour which twice each day fills the Los Angeles freeway system beyond capacity has brought traffic to a near standstill in the oppressive midsummer heat. A giant with severe emphysema, the city is exhaling the cause of its disease with only the greatest of difficulty.

"It's slow-and-go on the San Diego freeway northbound from the Santa Monica freeway to Ventura," reports radio station KNX traffic central. "The Santa Monica freeway westbound is slow-and-go from the Harbor freeway to Lincoln.

"There's a mattress reported on the San Bernadino freeway eastbound lane, and we have a report of a lady walking against the traffic on the southbound side of the Santa Ana freeway just south of the Long Beach interchange. Apparently the hood blew off her car and she's walking back to try and pull it out of the roadway.

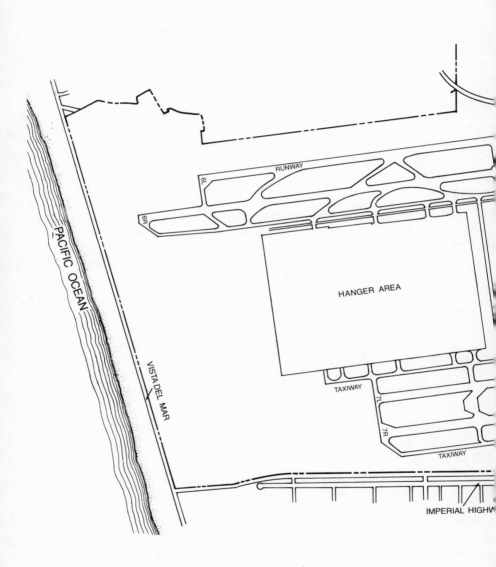

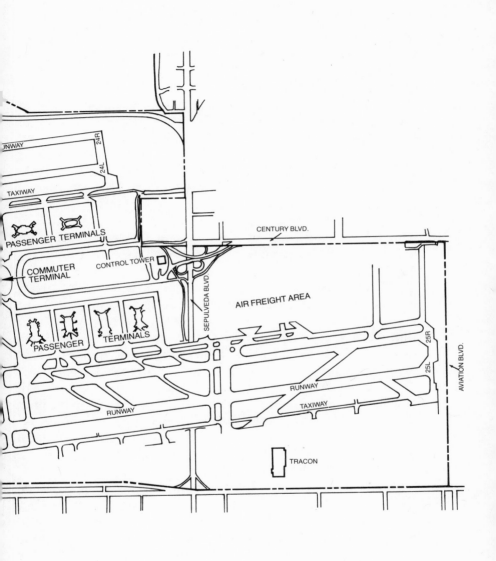

There's a black and white on the way to the scene, but you might keep an eye out for her."

From the glassed-in "cab" at the top of the 172-foot control tower located between LAX's four, parallel jet runways, autos moving to and from the airport along Century Boulevard between its main entrance and the San Diego freeway, a mile to the east, appear to be completely stalled.

Just south of the tower, but seeming more distant when viewed through the yellow-brown pollution which restricts visibility to less than three miles, LAX's two longest runways stretch 12,000 feet on a heading of 250 degrees to within less than a mile of the dense fog bank which marks the edge of the Pacific Ocean. Runway 25 is less than 1,500 feet from the tower. The centerline of runway 25 Left is a mere 800 feet south of runway 25 Right. About 1,500 feet north of the tower, runways 24 Left (10,285' by 150') and 24 Right (8,925 by 150') are similarly close to each other and to the 1,000-foot high fog bank which lies heavy and grey upon the ocean.

Though detached from the stop-and-go traffic on the streets below, the seven air traffic controllers now on duty in LAX tower are coping with a rush hour of their own. Twenty-three of the thirty-eight airlines which regularly serve the airport publish timetables which promise arrival at LAX within a few minutes of 5:00 P.M. Five flights—Northwest Orient 22, Western 443, United 523, Pacific Southwest 362, and United 114—are all scheduled to touch down at exactly 5:10 P.M. There will be more than forty landings here this hour and almost as many takeoffs—more than one takeoff or landing per minute—and the pace will continue until almost sunset. After that, when things are slow, there will be one landing or takeoff every ninety seconds until nearly 1:00 A.M.

Air traffic inbound to LAX from the east stretches single file for more than fifty miles, with a three-mile separation between planes like DC-9s, DC-707s, and DC-727s, and a five-mile separation between a jumbo jet and any following airliner because of the air turbulence generated by the jumbos. Until handed off to the tower when they're about seven miles east of the airport, these planes "belong" to a radar approach controller seated in another building on the south side of the airport. Farther to the east, in a highspeed, three-dimensional chess game not unlike the function performed at a railroad marshalling yard, other controllers are sequencing three converging lines of planes into the single file of airliners now streaming westward toward LAX.

Arrivals from the south are also under the jurisdiction of the controller handling arrivals from the east. Using speed control and coordination with other controllers in the "marshalling yard" (Los Angeles Center, at Palmdale), he builds *holes*—longer than the regulation spaces in the line of westward moving inbounds— into which he fits, at several hundred miles an hour, the unevenly spaced airliners headed north for landing at LAX.

A second approach controller, also across the field and seated near the controller handling east arrivals, blends converging lines of north and west arrivals into a second stream of inbounds headed east, just a few miles north of LAX. One by one, each will be "U-turned" to the right in a pattern similar to the design of a paper clip, and headed west, on a close parallel to LAX's east arrivals, toward the airport.

Under ideal, but almost never attainable, conditions, the stream of north and west arrivals would be landed on runways 24 Left and 24 Right, just north of the tower, and the stream of east arrivals would be landed on runways 25 Left and 25 Right, about a thousand yards south of the tower. But only one of the south runways, 25 Left, can take the weight of heavy jumbos, and 24 Right, close to hundreds of houses built after the runway was put into use, is restricted by noise abatement requirements.

Neither of the south runways is practical for foreign arrivals, since LAX's international terminal is located on the north side of the field.

Getting to the international terminal from the south side of the airport adds traffic to LAX's two congested north-south taxiways, often occupied by airliners arriving and departing the airport's commuter air terminal located between the north and south terminal complexes. Finally, departures from runways on both sides of the airport must be sequenced between frequent arrivals.

More than two thousand planes will land and takeoff here today. Before the year is out, more than 495,000 will have touched down at, and departed from, LAX's runways. They will have carried 24,000,000 passengers (more than the combined population of half the fifty states) and moved 1,250,000,000 pounds of freight (more than five pounds for every man, woman, and child in the United States) and 190,000,000 pounds of mail (a weight equal to fifteen ordinary letters for every individual in the nation).

Unlike the stop-and-go traffic on the freeways and streets below the tower, the hundreds of jets now inbound to LAX can neither stop nor back up. There is no way to stem the flow of inbounds—and precious little room to maneuver them—for crowded into the narrow confines of the Los Angeles basin are four of the nation's other seven busiest airports.

5 No Piece of Cake

You see people for what they are here. When you're on a busy position there's no front, absolutely nothing. Everything hangs out because you're only aware of what you're trying to do, which is separate airplanes. You're not aware of other things that you're doing such as your leg jerking, or your hand shaking, or having two cigarettes going at the same time, or squirming around in your chair.

CONGESTED AS it is with more than 495,000 landings and takeoffs a year, Los Angeles International Airport falls far short of being the busiest airport in the crowded, 40- by 100-mile Los Angeles basin.

Just thirty-five miles south of LAX, a few minutes as the jet flies, is Orange County Airport, second busiest airport in the United States (LAX is number seven) with 648,000 landings and takeoffs a year. Only Chicago O'Hare, busiest airport in the world, has more air traffic than Orange County.

Almost exactly half-way between Orange County and LAX, lies Long Beach Airport, fourth busiest in the entire United States,

43

with 540,000 landings and takeoffs each year.

Van Nuys Airport, third busiest in the nation with close to 610,000 landings and takeoffs annually, is a mere fifteen miles north of LAX's runways. Closer to LAX than any of these—twelve miles to the southwest—is Torrance, thirteenth busiest airport in the United States, but still with more air traffic than JFK, Washington National, San Francisco, LaGuardia, Miami International, Newark, or sprawling Dallas–Ft. Worth.

Also within the radius of a circle which would just touch Orange County Airport thirty-five miles south of LAX are eleven additional airports, six of which each handle more air traffic than the major airports of Oklahoma City, Cleveland, St. Paul, Buffalo, Minneapolis, and Tampa. Taken together, their traffic is more than twice that of Los Angeles International itself.

Thus, at any moment, nearly one-fourth of the total number of aircraft aloft over the more than 3,000,000 square miles of forty-eight contiguous states, are in the small airspace above the densely-populated and often smog-filled Los Angeles basin.

Surrounding Los Angeles International, and designed mainly to separate its 350,000 yearly airline flights from other traffic, is a piece of airspace shaped like an upside-down wedding cake. The smallest tier, centered on Los Angeles International, is five miles across and 2,000 feet high; the middle three tiers are more than twenty-five miles across and 2,000 feet thick, reaching from 2,000 to 4,000 feet above the ground; and finally, balanced on top, the largest tier is fifty miles across and 3,000 feet thick. Its base, resting on the two lower layers, is 4,000 feet above ground and its top touches 7,000 feet.

LAX's protective upside-down wedding cake isn't a perfect circle. Slices removed from the northern and southern portions reduce its north-south dimensions to about fifty miles. And bites have been taken out here and there to allow access to other airports under the shadow, but not the jurisdiction, of the terminal control area (TCA), which no plane may enter without clearance from a Los Angeles air traffic controller.

Beyond the required clearance for entry, there is what aviation

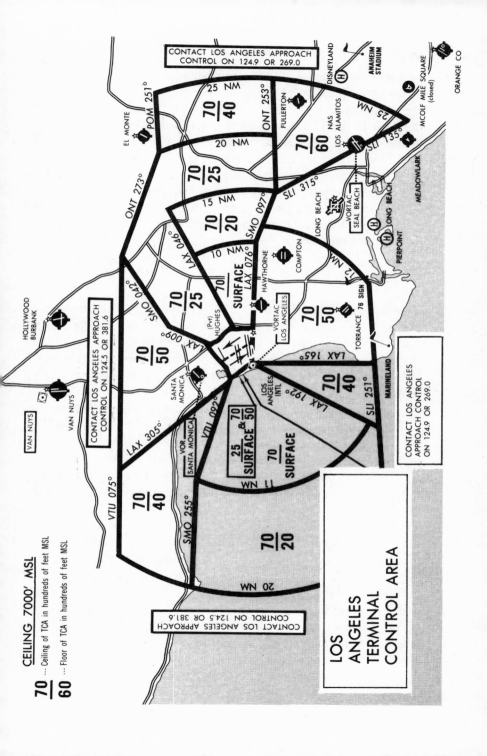

people have come to call "the price of admission," the expense of a two-way radio, radio navigational equipment, and an altitude-reporting transponder. The critical part of the key which unlocks the door to the TCA is a plane's transponder, for, at every sweep of the rotating FAA radar antenna, the transponder talks to the LAX approach control computer, telling it the plane's registration number (or airline flight number), position, altitude, and ground-speed. The computer displays this information in what controllers call a "data block" close to each plane, called a "target," on the radarscope. A typical data block, displayed in glowing green numbers on the radarscope, looks like this:

TW 229
120 23

That is, TWA flight 229, at 12,000 feet, flying at 230 knots—about 265 mph. Whenever a plane's speed, position, or altitude change, the transponder tells the computer—and the computer updates the data block. And wherever each plane goes, its data block follows, so the controller has a pretty good picture of what's going on in his sector of airspace.

Non-transponder targets—planes without transponders—are visible on the radarscope most of the time, but not always.

The FAA's radar and computers work well together in displaying aircraft and their following data blocks—most of the time.

The controllers' radios used for communicating with planes moving at hundreds of miles an hour work quite well—most of the time.

But, during the random moments each day when equipment fails, a Los Angeles controller working fifteen or twenty airplanes in close proximity to each other is suddenly struck deaf and dumb —or blind—without warning. It is then that his heart races and his chest tightens and his stomach muscles constrict and his blood pressure soars in what has been medically described as a feeling of helplessness and impending disaster which generates more stress than man was built to endure.

6   Local One

You hear a controller talk: clear to land; clear to takeoff; follow the DC-9 for runway 25 Right; turn off at the first high speed taxiway; do this do that—and you think, 'Gee that's not so bad,' because you're just hearing a monotone. But what you're not hearing is what's going on inside his head or how he feels, like, 'God damn, I hope this works; now that better *work; if he doesn't do that I'm gonna have to do this.' You gotta constantly have a plan for what you're gonna do if each one goofs.*

VINNIE LAMPTON is working local one, the tower position which handles landings and takeoffs from runways 25 Left and 25 Right. He's standing at the southeast corner of the tower cab. Over at the cab's northeast corner, another controller is working local two (runways 24 Left and 24 Right). Between Vinnie and the local two controller is a teleprinter clicking out flight plans which will be assigned to departing flights before takeoff. The position is called *clearance delivery* and nobody likes to work it. "CD" is the position new people are started on—and you're not moving airplanes, just handling paper. On Vinnie's right, when he's facing runways 25 Left and 25 Right to the west, is the ground controller who, as the term suggests, controls planes moving on the ground which are taxiing to and from the terminal gates, the runways, the freight terminals, and the maintenance hangars. More trainees at LAX tower wash out on ground control than on any other position. It's like one of those two-and-a-half-inch square puzzles, where you have fifteen squares with numbers on them and only one empty space and you try to slide the numbers around to get them in order, only you're working with airplanes and you don't have time to stop and ponder.

The supervisor's desk is in the southwest corner of the cab; the stairs from below are in the northwest corner. There's a second ground control position near the top of the stairs, just left of the local two position, but the shift is short-handed so the one controller is working both ground positions. A new man, an experienced controller transferred from Las Vegas tower, is studying procedures with the supervisor.

Vinnie was due for a break at 5:00. For the past ten minutes he's been giving Ron Fraser, the controller who's about to relieve him, a rundown on traffic inbound to runways 25 Left and 25 Right plus the list of departures he's holding for takeoff near the approach ends of the runways. Fraser's earphone and boom microphone have also been plugged into a set of jacks adjacent to Vinnie's; he's heard everything which Vinnie has said and done. "O.K., buddy, you got it?" asks Vinnie. "I just cleared American three zero six for two five Right, he's just about to touch down. The first one out there on final is Northwest twenty-two; he's goin' to two four Left so you don't have to worry about him. You got United five twenty-three and PSA three sixty-two inbound. United five twenty-two and American four seventy-two are one and two for departure on two five Right. It's all yours."

At the moment Fraser takes over local one, there are twenty-seven airliners inbound to the position's two runways, and eight planes lined up for takeoff. Counting average load factors for the additional planes he'll handle during the next hour, Fraser has accepted, with nothing more formal than a nod, air traffic responsibility for more than 18,000 lives—all depending upon his fault-less memory, spilt-second judgement, and ability to remain calm under almost any conditions. For sixty minutes, give or take a few, Fraser will work in perfect concert with the ground controller for his two runways, and with an approach controller on the other side of the airport who feeds him his traffic at the rate of 200 lives every forty seconds.

Fraser must sense, from the pilots' vocal mannerisms how sharp and experienced they are so that he will have a feel for what he can count on if he has to issue a last-minute runway change or snap out emergency instructions. Every few seconds, and with the subconscious expertise with which a racing driver shifts gears, he will check the downwind ends of his runways to make sure they're clear. And he will sense, listening with the ear not covered by his headset, the tension level of the ground controller. If his ground controller's voice shows any hint of concern, Fraser will take "plenty of time, two or three seconds," to examine the ground situation before he clears another plane to land. And, by watching on his radarscope how smoothly Fraser handles each pitch he tosses him, the approach controller on the other side of the field will know if he can safely keep the traffic coming, or if he'll be forced to ask the en route center to begin circling airplanes—out over Arizona somewhere—to give the tower a breathing spell.

"Western four forty-three's at Lima," reports Fraser's first inbound, a 727 passing over a radio fix five and a half miles east of LAX's two south runways.

"*Western four forty-three, Los Angeles, two five Right, clear to land,*" replies Fraser. "*Wind's* [from] *two six zero* [degrees] *at ten knots.*" Without having to think about it, he has confirmed that the pilot is tuned to Los Angeles and not to one of the thirteen other airports in the Los Angeles basin.

"Cleared for two five Right, Western four forty-three," affirms the pilot. An unacknowledged instruction is the same as one not given, and must be repeated by the controller until acknowledged.

"*American three zero six,*" continues Fraser to an airliner which has just touched down on the runway he's cleared Western

443 to land on, *"first available high speed turnoff please, traffic on short final; contact ground point seven five* [121.75], *clearing."*

"American three zero six," the pilot acknowledges.

"United five twenty-two, two five Right, cleared for immediate [takeoff]; *maintain two* [thousand]; *expect higher* [altitude] *from departure. Wind two six zero at ten."*

"United five twenty-two," replies the pilot, simultaneously turning onto the runway and applying full power.

As United 522 begins its takeoff roll, Fraser presses one of a cluster of twenty buttons on his communications console, buttons which can instantly connect his microphone and earphones via telephone line with a score of other air traffic control positions in the area. "United five twenty-two's off two five Right to maintain two," he advises a departure controller seated at a radarscope in a building on the south side of the field.

As the departure controller says, "O.K., we got 'em," the transponder-computer-radar link which identifies every plane arriving or departing LAX displays United 522's data block on the radarscope:

UA 522

020 13

and United 522 climbs through 2,000 feet at 130 knots.

Once the departure controller confirms he "has" United 522, Fraser "hands off" the flight to the departure controller's radio frequency:

"United five twenty-two, contact departure now one two four point three."

"Two four three. So long now."

"Have a good one."

"American three zero six clear two five Right; gate eight three," announces the airliner which has just cleared that runway.

"Ground [control] *point seven five, sir,"* replies Fraser to the American pilot who has failed to switch from the local one frequency to ground control.

"Sorry 'bout that, American three zero six."

"American four seventy-two, it's going to be a few minutes before I can get you out."

"Four seventy-two," the American pilot replies, knowing that a wait of several minutes is required before he can safely be cleared to take off behind United 522, a turbulence-generating jumbo jet.

Standing close to Ron Fraser, a new controller recently transferred from another airport observes how Fraser handles local one. The new man's boom microphone and single earphone headset are plugged into the local one position so that he can hear everything said by Fraser and the aircraft he's talking to. There's no loudspeaker turned on in the tower because several controllers —local one, local two, helicopter control, ground control, and clearance delivery—are all talking to different airplanes at the same time.

"Baron eight whiskey mike's with you, Lima," calls a small twin-engine private plane.

"O.K. eight whiskey mike, Los Angeles, two five Left, clear to land. Wind's two six zero at ten."

"Eight whiskey mike, cleared two five Left."

"Los Angeles, United five twenty-three's with you inside Lima."

"United five twenty-three, Los Angeles, clear to land two five Right. Wind two six zero at ten."

"Five twenty-three for the Right."

"United five twenty-three, first available [turnoff] *please. Ground point seven five."*

"United five twenty-three."

"American four seventy-two, two five Right, position and hold; be ready for immediate."

"American four seventy-two."

"Los Angeles, United 114 heavy (a DC-10), Lima."

"United one fourteen, Los Angeles, cleared two five Left. Wind two six zero at ten."

"United one fourteen."

"American four seventy-two, two five Right, cleared for takeoff,

maintain two, expect higher from departure. Have a good flight."

"American four seventy-two, maintain two thousand, so long."

"Eight whiskey mike, first left turnoff please. Where are you going?"

"Butler Aviation."

"O.K., it's the big blue and white sign there. Contact ground point seven five clearing."

"Eight whiskey mike."

"American four seventy-two, contact departure one two four point three."

"Departure one two four point three, American four seventy-two."

"United one fourteen, second high speed turnoff, hold short of two five Right."

"Second turnoff and hold short of two five Right, United one fourteen."

"Los Angeles, United eight fifty-seven, Lima."

"United one fourteen, clear to cross two five Right, contact ground point seven five clearing."

"United one fourteen's clear to cross, ground point seven five."

"United eight fifty-seven, Los Angeles, two five Right, cleared to land; wind two six zero at ten."

"United eight fifty-seven for Right."

"O.K. American two twenty-one, two five Left, position and hold."

"American two twenty-one."

"American two zero two [holding short of] two five Right, we'll get you off in a couple of minutes."

"American two zero two."

"What I'm trying to do," explains Fraser to the new man during a brief pause in the almost constant stream of arriving traffic, "is to land as many airliners as possible on two five Right, which is closest to the passenger terminals just north of the runway."

"United eight fifty-seven," Fraser tells a Boeing 727 just touch-

ing down on 25 Right, *"first available turnoff please, traffic on short final. Contact ground point seven five clearing."*

"United eight fifty-seven off at the next high speed, ground seven five."

As United 857 clears the runway, Fraser tells the pilot of American 202, *"American two zero two [holding short of], two five Right, cleared for immediate takeoff."*

"Cleared for immediate, American two zero two."

Barely a minute after American 202's departure, Fraser clears American 221 for takeoff from 25 Left. Ninety seconds later, Hughesair 847 touches down on the same runway.

"Hughesair eight forty-seven, second turnoff please. Hold short of two five Right."

"Hughesair eight forty-seven, short of two five Right."

"I have to land all the wide bodies I get; DC-10s and L-1011s, on two five Left because two five Right can't take the weight. That means all the wide bodies you land have to hold on a taxiway between two five Left and two five Right, until two five Right is free enough to clear them across it to the terminals.

"Besides the wide bodies which have to land on two five Left for noise abatement, I also want to land as many of the private planes there as possible because two five Left is closest to their terminals on the south side of the field. Finally, anything that weighs more than 320,000 pounds—that includes all 747s and some heavily-loaded DC-10s and L-1011s—*must* be landed on two four Right because it's the only runway we've got that's stressed to take the weight.

"We also try to put as many southbound departures as we can on two five Left for takeoff. If your southbounds take off from two five Right, then they'll have to cross the two five Left departure course when they're turned left to go southbound. So put southbounds on two five Left to avoid that, then you can depart planes simultaneously on two five Left and two five Right—so long as your two five Left departure isn't going northbound. Got that?"

"Los Angeles, Western four zero eight, Lima."

"Western four zero eight, Los Angeles, two five Right, cleared to land. Wind's two six zero at ten."

"Now, most of our departures from the runway two five complex take off from two five Right, but if you're backed up like we often are, you can scoot 'em across the approach end of two five Right and hold 'em short of two five Left between the runways for departure from two five Left. *Or* you can coordinate with ground control and squeak 'em across the far end of two five Right and two five Left and bring 'em up on the long parallel taxiway to the south of two five Left."

"Los Angeles, Western sixty-three, Lima."

"Western sixty-three, Los Angeles, two five Right cleared to land, wind two six zero at ten; company traffic just touching down.

"Western four zero eight, first high speed turnoff please, company traffic [on] *short final. Ground point seven five clearing."*

"Western four zero eight clearing."

"Los Angeles, American one nineteen, Lima."

"American one nineteen, two five Right, clear to land. Wind two six zero at ten."

"Cleared for the Right, American one nineteen."

"American six zero three, two five Left, clear for takeoff, maintain two, expect higher. Wind two six zero at ten."

"American six zero three."

"Western sixty-three, the first high speed please, ground point seven five clearing."

"Western sixty-three."

5:32 P.M. During the past twenty minutes, while he's been training Ted Merril, Fraser has worked ten airplanes for landing and two for departure. If traffic continues at its present rate for the next hour—which Fraser can expect during the evening arrival rush—he will have worked thirty-six to forty airplanes by the time he's due to be relieved. An additional duty during that time will be to to continue training the new man.

After a twenty-minute break, if he isn't the one who's sent out to bring in food, he'll rotate to other positions: helicopter control, clearance delivery, ground control, and, before he goes off duty, local two.

7 Ron Fraser

I became enraptured with air traffic control when I started in the Air Force in 1966. I love it and I think most of us do. Maybe it's an ego thing, maybe the power you have or the excitement of an airport like LAX. The first minute you're in the cab you can sense that everyone works together very well, most cooperate without even a verbal request.

WE WERE having lunch in the LAX employees' cafeteria at ground level beneath the circular restaurant atop a modernistic platform suspended from stressed concrete arches in the center of the terminal area. The cafeteria food comes from the same kitchen as the restaurant food, and you can save 30 percent if you can stand the atmosphere. It's not all that bad, and most of the stewardesses eat there—which is reason enough for most of the tower controllers to eat there too when they have a chance to get off the position for thirty minutes or so.

It used to be, before the 1976 union contract which liberalized clothing requirements, that you could always spot air traffic controllers in the cafeteria because of the FAA's former IBM-style dress code. Airline crews were in uniform and ticket agents wore a company tie and blazer, so any male between twenty-five and thirty-five wearing a shirt and tie was an air traffic controller. Today, though, Ron Fraser is wearing Levi's, a tan shirt, and sneakers. His dark hair and beard, and powerful, five-foot, ten-inch build would look perfectly in place on the deck of a schooner at sea.

"You've always got to be thinking ahead every minute, because, whatever happens, you've got to handle it. Nobody else can help, it's all moving too fast and you're the only one who has the picture. It can jump up and bite you any time.

"A while ago I had this big L-1011 making an approach under emergency conditions. He was heavy, full of fuel, and had an engine out. I had issued him a landing runway, which was 24 Left. I was diverted from watching him for just a few seconds because of the other traffic I was working and when I looked back at him he was less than half a mile from touching down on 24 *Right,* which was a closed runway with about fifty or sixty men working on it, as well as trucks and bulldozers. "I told him, 'Immediate go-around!' and he said, 'Negative! We're emergency!' and I said, 'Don't land there, that runway's closed!' And he came within maybe fifty feet of landing. I could see men hitting the deck, it was that close. I'd say we were fifteen seconds from disaster.

"Then there's just the other day. We had this Flying Tiger cargo jet ready to depart 25 Right and we had a TWA L-1011 landing on 25 Left. The guy working local one cleared the L-1011 to cross 25 Right and then cleared the Tiger for takeoff. "In the meantime, a United DC-10 pulled out and blocked the taxiway the L-1011 needed to clear 25 Right—and Tiger had to jump him. Tiger was rolling when United blocked the TWA and there was no way Tiger could have stopped. He really didn't quite have flying speed yet, so when he jumped the L-1011 he came back down again and going down the runway his tail left a trail of sparks for a hundred feet or so; just scared the hell out of me, but he finally got it into the air. "When Tiger called the tower, the local one controller said, 'Hey Tiger, I'm really sorry about that;

I was counting on TWA to clear.' and the Tiger pilot tells him, 'My fault all the way.' He never said another word.

"I'm an aggressive controller and the faster the traffic moves, the better I like it. I don't know of any other area where people work in such close proximity under such pressure for such a long time; a surgeon maybe, but the operation doesn't usually last that long; or cops, but they spend a lot of time just riding around.

"During the rushes a decision by one man has to be backed by another man. Like when the local controller has a fast influx of arrivals, he's got to have a close relationship with the ground controller so that the ground controller doesn't have an airplane right in the middle of a taxiway he needs to use to clear the runway. The controller working local has to depend on the ground controller's knowing how to work local as well as he knows how to work ground control. And of course I have to know the ground controller's job, too, so I can anticipate what he's going to do. As he starts planes up toward the departure end of the runway I start formulating my plan, like, 'That one there's southbound so I can depart him from the south runway,' or, 'He's a heavy cargoliner so he's going to need longer to get off,' or, 'That's a jumbo and I'm gonna have to wait three minutes before I can depart another one behind him.'

"As much as possible you can't let yourself count on anything until you see it happen. A plane lands and you tell him, 'First available taxiway please, traffic on short final,' and he says, 'Roger'; you can't just turn your eyes off of him as he rolls past the tower. You have to make sure he's off the runway before you clear the next one to land. Usually you watch them roll out and if you don't see smoke coming from the wheels you can count on them clearing; but each time you have to make sure.

"TWA's bad about that a lot of the time. Their terminal is just to the right of the far end of 25 Right so you tell them to make the first available turn off and they say 'Roger' and then sail right on past it. They do that because they don't want to turn off, maybe hold on the turn-off for a minute and then taxi slowly all the way down to their gate. So you have to watch TWA a little more than you do some of the others.

"When I came here from Ontario [California] TRACON [Terminal Radar Control] a couple of years ago, I didn't know if I would be able to make it because of LAX's reputation for high standards. I was a radar [approach and departure] controller at Ontario, so working in the tower at LAX would be something new. I went through the training program O.K. You have to prove yourself. You have to take a lot of ribbing; they push you just to see how much you can take and they'll leave you on combined positions, like local one and two, which hardly anybody can handle, just to see where you fall apart. Not that it's all that uptight either. Except for when it's very, very busy we joke and kid around a lot. I think it's like with the surgeons in an operating room; you do it to stay loose so you're free to flow easy and handle whatever comes up. And when there's time, like late at night, we kid around with the pilots too.

"PSA [Pacific Southwest Airlines] comes in and outta here a hundred times a day and we got word that this new pilot was making his first trip into LAX, so every time the local one man talks to him one of the other controllers keys his microphone at the same time and goes, 'Mmmmmmmmmmmm' while the local one man is talking to him.

"Finally the local one man says, 'PSA nine twenty-eight, you seem to have a hum in your microphone,' and PSA says, 'Yeah, you seem to have a hum too. I better have the radio checked.'

"And sometimes we sort of drop the standard aviation phraseology, too. Like the other night one of the Delta cargo flights calls us and says, 'Hey Los Angeles, Delta flight number so and so, got your ears on?' and the local one man answers him, 'That's a big 10-4, good buddy. Say your 10-20.' And Delta says 'Lima' and the local one man tells him, 'Freight crate, you're cleared to drop and stop your flight on the 25 Right.'

"Even trying to lighten things as much as you can, it's still impossible to be keyed up for this kind of operation for eight hours and go home and after only four or five hours be able to go to bed and drift off into a period of sound, restful sleep and then come back and do it all over again. I've had nights where I just awake in the middle of the night sweating because of nightmares about a mid-air or a near mid-air. I have lots of friends who drink pretty heavily to soften the day's stress, but for me it just takes time to slow down. I go home and do some activity like gardening until I settle down. The majority of controllers, I believe, tend to take a shortcut. Not that all of us are alcoholics by any means, but a lot go out for a drink after work to talk it over with the guys who were there with them.

"If you were to ask me about the worst part of the job I would have to say it's worrying about my family. I always have nightmares about coming home late at night or in the morning after I'm off the midwatch and somehow finding my family hurt or injured. The rotating shift work and the stress is bad on your family in a lot of ways. I'm too drained from the job when I get home and I'm too tired to sit down and talk about decisions, so running the home is pretty much up to my wife. It puts a load on her. I walk in and all I want is for my wife to understand that I've had a hard day, but it seems every time you take your wife to visit the facility it's an especially light day and all she sees is seven people standing around doing nothing.

"I feel like I short-change my family a lot and sometimes it's really hard to leave for work when she doesn't want you to and she's asking why you can't 'sick-out' or something. She really hates for me to leave her and the kids alone at 10:00 P.M. to work the midwatch. The midwatch from eleven at night to seven in the morning is especially bad. You've just gotten off duty at three that same afternoon and with driving time you're lucky to get five hours rest.

"After midnight, because of noise abatement regulations, we have to make all landings to the east and all takeoffs to the west, using the inboard runways, so what you often have is a plane taking off heading west, and another plane eastbound on final approach for landing, facing head-on with the departing plane.

"When you add that to the fact that the controllers have had maybe four or five hours sleep, and that a lot of those planes are being flown by pilots just getting here after a long overseas flight —many of them foreigners who don't understand English too well —you're asking for trouble. Sooner or later we'll have a mid-air and they'll say to hell with the noise abatement regulations and we'll change things. But that's what it will take. It always does.

"I have to say that I like training. I enjoy it because I feel I know my job well and feel I can pass on what I know to someone else here. You've got to make a trainee think. You've got to let him go as far as you safely can without jumping on his back. Nobody comes to LAX off the street. Any trainee who comes here is an experienced controller. You can't sit on him because he's got to develop his own feel for the situation, not somebody else's feel. You have to know the other person's style of working traffic and respect it."

8   The New Man

Starting at LAX was just as bad as I thought it would be. I knew when I came here it would be rough, and it really is. Those guys are the best there is and they demand a lot. The first week was really terrible and I wondered if I did the right thing coming here. It's a big change if you haven't worked airliners before. I stood there in awe at the size of those 747s compared to the little Cessnas and Pipers I'd been working.

IN THE northeast and southeast corners of the twelve-by-twelve-foot tower cab, hanging from the ceiling just above the local one and local two positions, on tracks like spotlights in an art gallery, are two radarscopes, each in a separate sixteen-by-sixteen-inch box which can be turned any direction. The two radars' air traffic picture is the same one shown on the approach and departure controllers' radarscopes in the TRACON (Terminal Radar Control) building across the field, except that here the range is set for twelve miles, compared with the fifty-mile working range used by approach and departure controllers. On the tower radars, there are computer-generated symbols showing the locations of nearby airports, radio navigational aids, prominent landmarks, and reporting points which every tower controller must memorize.

It's 4:40 P.M. and Joe Gibbs, tower supervisor this watch, has turned the local two radarscope toward the center of the room. He's standing with Ted Merril, the new man, using a pointer which he touches to symbols on the radar display:

"O.K.," Gibbs says, touching a small, open, bright circle like a perfect "O," "what's this?"

"That's Hughes Airport."

"And this one up here; what's this?"

"That's Hawthorne Airport."

"What's this?"

"That one I'm not familiar with."

"How about this one here?"

"The diamond?"

"Yeah"

"That's stadium."

"How about this one?"

"That's coliseum."

"You haven't got one right yet. Here's stadium; stadium and coliseum are the same thing. All right, this diamond here is Crenshaw Square. The lower diamond here is Rosecranz Boulevard. This one up here is Wilshire and Western. All these are frequently-called reporting points.

"Hughes Airport is this circle just north of LAX; this one up here is Santa Monica Airport. Do you know where the Yellow River runs?"

"No."

"O.K. It runs east and turns at Downey and then goes almost straight north.

"Do you know where Downey is?"

"Yes."

Handing Merril the pointer, "Show me."

"Here," replies Merril, touching the pointer to the radarscopes's protective glass.

"Right. This down here is the San Diego Freeway; this is Harbor Freeway. Here's Long Beach Airport; here's Torrance.

"When we're on the midwatch in a couple days I'll put the radar on longer range and you'll see Silver Lake up north and the Hollywood Bowl, but the most important ones you're seeing now. Alamo Park isn't on the map any more; it should be; it's right here.

"Remember: here's stadium, here's Santa Monica, here's Hughes, here's Hawthorne, here's—what?"

"Torrance."

"Right."

Two and half hours ago, when he'd finished quizzing Merril, Gibbs pulled down the tinted, transparent shades along the glass wall on the west side of the tower cab. The arrival rush which began about 5:00 P.M. has tapered off now and the lowering sun, yellowed even more than a usual sunset by the thick pollution which hangs over the city, now shines almost directly through the cab.

"Hey, Merril," says one of the controllers to the five-foot, five-inch trainee, "now I know why you don't wear a name tag. It's because it would get caught in the shag carpet."

"Charlie," says Gibbs, "in a minute I'll have heard just about enough out of you!"

"Yeah, I know," answers Charlie, "that's why I'm saying it now."

Merril has been working ground control two, under supervision of one of the journeymen controllers, for the past hour. Now, with his headset plugged into local one so he doesn't miss a word, he'll be observing Ron Fraser for twenty minutes before working the position under Fraser's supervision.

Joe Gibbs has just updated the air traffic information service (ATIS) recording which is broadcast continuously to reduce the need for pilots and controllers to congest the already busy tower control frequencies by asking for and receiving routine information.

"Los Angeles arrival information *Hotel,*" intones Gibbs' recorded voice, "02:45 [Greenwich] weather: clear, smoke, haze; visibility four; temperature eight seven; dew point seven five; wind two five zero degrees at five; altimeter two nine point nine six. Simultaneous instrument approaches in progress runways 24 Left and 25 Left. All aircraft advise approach control on initial contact that you have information *Hotel.*

"Los Angeles arrival information *Hotel* . . ." continues the endless tape as Joe cuts off the speaker he'd used to monitor the recording. It will be updated any time there's a significant change in the weather or airport condition.

As a landing airliner passes over the fence at the approach end of runway 25 Left, moving at 140 mph and still several hundred feet in the air, Ron Fraser clears another plane onto the approach end of the runway:

"*Western five fourteen, two five Left, position and hold.*"

"Western five fourteen, position and hold."

"What I did," Fraser advises Merril, still not turning his attention away from the runways, "was give the Western 'position and hold' before the other plane touches down. You can do that because, by the time Western's engines get up to speed, anybody who's landing will be beyond him and down the runway. You can save two or three minutes that way.

"*Western five fourteen, two five Left, clear for takeoff. Wind two five zero at five.*"

"Western five fourteen, so long."

"O.K., Ted," says Fraser, stepping back from the local one position a bit, "you've got it."

"*PSA three forty-eight,*" Merril directs the pink and coral Southwest Pacific Airlines Boeing 727 holding short of the approach end of 25 Right, "*cross two five Right, hold short of two five Left.*"

"PSA three forty-eight," acknowledges the airliner responding quickly to Merril's instruction. With five years behind him in other towers, the new man manages to sound as confident and authoritative as any seasoned controller at LAX tower.

"*PSA three forty-eight, two five Left, position and hold now,*" Merril adds as Delta 622, a huge L-1011 previously cleared to land by Ron Fraser, passes over the end of the runway.

"Position and hold, three forty-eight."

"Delta six twenty-two, second high speed turnoff please, clear to cross two five Right, contact ground point seven five, clearing two five Right."

"Delta six twenty-two."

"O.K., Ted, let's clear three forty-eight; you've got traffic on final for two five Left."

"PSA three forty-eight, two five Left, clear for immediate [takeoff]; *maintain two. Wind two six zero at nine."*

With PSA 348 rolling, Fraser makes the rundown to departure control and hands the flight off to the departure controller: *"PSA three forty-eight, contact departure now one two four point three. So long."*

"Hughesair seven eighty-five's ready," reports a yellow DC-9 at the approach end of 25 Right.

"Hughesair seven eighty-five, hold short of two five Right."

"Los Angeles, PSA seven twenty-six, Lima."

"PSA seven twenty-six, Los Angeles, two five Right, clear to land. Wind two six zero at nine."

"PSA seven twenty-six, clear for the right."

"Ted, which runway do you think is the best one for Hughesair seven eighty-five to get off on?"

"The left?"

"No, the right. Look at the radar; Hughesair eight is right on the tail of Western eight thirteen for two five Left, so you can't get seven eighty-five off on the left. So two five Right is the first runway you can use for departure."

"PSA seven twenty-six," Merril says to the 727 just touching down on 25 Right, *"right turn, ground point seven five clearing."*

"Cut your verbiage down, Ted. There's no reason to tell PSA to turn *right:* he's obviously not going to turn left and cross two five Left and go over to the private plane terminals or something. O.K., let's get Hughesair seven eighty-five into position."

"Hughesair seven eighty-five, two five Right, taxi into position and hold."

"Seven eighty-five."

"Again, Ted, keep your verbiage down, you don't have to say *taxi* into position; how else would he get there? Actually, you don't have to say *into* either; just *position and hold.*

"Now who's next behind seven eighty-five? Get your plan made. It's a Braniff, right? Ask him if you don't know who it is."

"Braniff nine zero eight, you number two?"

"Affirm, nine zero eight."

"Los Angeles, Western eight thirteen, Lima for two five."

"Western eight thirteen, Los Angeles, clear to land two five Left. Wind two six zero at nine."

"Western eight thirteen."

"Los Angeles, Hughesair eight, Lima."

"Hughesair eight, Los Angeles, two five Left, clear to land. Wind two six zero at nine."

"Hughesair eight."

"Western eight thirteen," Merril tells the red and white 727 rolling out on 25 Left, *"first available turnoff please, traffic on final. Clear to cross two five Right, contact ground point seven five clearing."*

"Western eight thirteen, clear to cross two five Right, ground point seven five."

"O.K., Hughesair eight, first available and you're also cleared to cross two five Right, [contact] *ground* [control] *clearing."*

"Hughesair eight."

"O.K., Ted, let's get ready to clear Hughesair seven eighty-five just as soon as the other Hughesair clears two five Right."

Before the new man has a chance to depart Hughesair 785, another arrival reports inbound over Lima:

"Los Angeles, PSA two eighty-four, Lima."

"Los Angeles, United three forty-five coming up on Lima," reports a wide-body DC-10 just a few miles behind PSA 284. His early call to the tower—before reaching Lima—is the DC-10 pilot's between-the-lines language for advising LAX tower that he's concerned about crowding PSA 284.

Finally, the frequency is quiet for the few seconds Merril needs to depart Hughesair:

"Hughesair seven eighty-five, two five Right, clear for takeoff. Wind two six zero at nine."

"Hughesair seven eighty-five rolling," responds the chrome-yellow DC-9 as it begins to move with increasing speed down the runway.

"O.K., Ted, go back to your traffic on final. Talk to them. Get United three forty-five slowed to his final approach speed, he's eating up PSA out there."

"PSA two eighty-four, two five Left, clear to land. Wind two six zero at nine.

"United three forty-five, Los Angeles, slow to your final approach speed please, continue for two five Left. Do you have the PSA 727 twelve o'clock four miles also for two five Left?"

"United three forty-five has the seven twenty-seven; slowing for two five Left."

Within the exchange between United 345 and LAX tower was this unspoken communication:

"United three forty-five, there's not much distance between you and that PSA seven twenty-seven up ahead and I'm kind of concerned about it. Could you please back off of him as much as possible. I'd sure appreciate it."

"Yeah, tower, we'll hang it out here as slow as we can and give little brother up there room to breathe. Don't sweat it."

The message, also heard by the pilot of the 727 just about to touch down, relieved some of the pressure he was feeling from the giant DC-10's proximity; a pressure which, in spite of everything, urged him to get his plane on the ground sooner, to slow it more abruptly, and to attempt to clear the runway more quickly than he normally would. Concern about the following DC-10 was now greatly reduced and he would make a better landing because of it.

"O.K., Ted, that was good," Fraser congratulates the new man. "You got PSA, who was closer to the runway, cleared to land before you talked to United. And you handled the other situation well too."

"PSA two eighty-four, second turnoff, hold short of two five Right.

"United three forty-five, two five Left, cleared to land. Wind two six zero at nine. Appreciate the help."

"No problem, United three forty-five for two five Left."

"Los Angeles, United seven twenty-one, Lima."

"United seven twenty-one, Los Angeles, two five Right, cleared to land. Wind two six zero at nine."

"United seven twenty-one, clear for two five Right."

"O.K., now you can get United three forty-five and PSA two eighty-four across two five Right before seven twenty-one gets here. Tell them now."

"United three forty-five, first available high speed turnoff please, clear to cross two five Right, company traffic on final for two five Right. Contact ground point seven five clearing the right.

"United three forty-five. We'll make the next one; ground point seven five clearing the right."

"O.K., now, PSA two eighty-four, after United three forty-five passes your position you're cleared to cross two five Right; ground point seven five. Traffic on final for two five Right."

"Clear to cross two five Right soon as the United is past us, PSA two eighty-four."

"That guy flying United three forty-five can land at my airport any time," says Merril, more comfortable working the position now that he's caught up in it.

"Yeah, well sometimes you get good ones like that."

"Los Angeles, Eastern eighty-three's inside Lima."

"Eastern eighty-three, Los Angeles, two five Right, continue approach. Your traffic's United seven twenty-seven, two-mile final [approach], *also for two five Right."*

"O.K., Ted, United seven twenty-one's touching down, get him primed and off the runway so you can clear Eastern."

"United seven twenty-one, first available turnoff please. Contact ground point seven five clearing." There's no response from United 721 which continues rolling down the runway.

"O.K., Ted, he's not acknowledging, so you've got to watch him to see if he's going to make the next turnoff. Get him committed!"

"United seven twenty-one," repeats Merril, allowing the barest hint of urgency to shade his voice, *"first available turnoff please, traffic short final. Contact ground point seven five clearing."*

"United seven twenty-one."

"O.K., buddy, take a break," Fraser tells the new man, "I'll work it for a while longer and then we'll grab a bite."

"Continental one twenty-six, Los Angeles," Fraser replies to a 727 reporting over Lima, *"two five Right, clear to land. Wind now two five zero at five."*

As Merril descends the stairs leading to the controllers' ready-room one flight below, he hears his instructor clear another plane to land, and another to take off, and another. . . . When the new man began his stint on local one, the setting sun was already below the horizon. Now, as the evening rush of traffic tapers to a manageable flow, the entire city seems to breathe more easily; the atmosphere of the tower cab, too, is changing. From a greenhouse with no apparent walls, at least in a psychological sense, the tower is becoming a more intimate, and somehow safer-feeling, place. The horizon moves in from a haze-hidden infinity to a middle-distance of office buildings, high-rise motels, and banks whose roof-mounted signs add warmth to the small, soft, rheostat-controlled spotlights recessed in the ceiling above each position.

A telephone rings and the watch supervisor picks up the direct line from approach and departure control across the field. "Yeah, you jug jugglers, what now?" he asks in the mock-sarcasm which colors much of the talk that passes between tower controllers and the TRACON's radar controllers on the south side of the airport.

"Hey, listen, you dum dum," retorts the TRACON controller "we got a Fairchild F-twenty-seven [twin-engine turboprop] inbound with an engine problem. Says he wants no emergency equipment and there will be no go-around. He's three four eight four Bravo."

"I'll tell *him* about the equipment, friend. So where is he and what's his downtime?"

"He's over Compton outta seven [thousand] so he should be there in about ten minutes. The readout shows him making one four zero knots."

"Passengers and fuel, friend?" asks Gibbs.

"O.K., he's got ten souls on board and an-hour-and-a-half fuel."

"O.K., give me a call when you're ready to hand him off [to us]; and tell him to plan on two five Left."

"O.K., buddy, two five Left."

"You ain't no buddy of mine, friend. Call me right back, O.K.?"

"Ten-four, good buddy."

"Hey, you guys," calls the watch supervisor over the voices of the controllers quietly working their positions, "we have an emergency inbound, an F-twenty-seven with an engine problem; ten souls on board and an-hour-and-a-half fuel; due in, in about ten minutes, for 25 Left.

"Ron, I told approach to tell him to expect two five Left; hope you don't mind my giving away your runway like that."

"No problem boss; I'll just send my inbound jumbos to Hawaii, they should be able to make it."

The supervisor phones Los Angeles Fire Department Engine Company 80 on the north end of the field and airport security. When the F-27 touches down, several fire engines and ambulances, permanently based on the airport, will be spaced along the runway to come to the plane's immediate assistance if needed.

To the south, the red rotating beacons atop the ambulances and fire engines are already visible as they head toward the wide grass area between runways 25 Left and 25 Right. There may be sirens, but we can't hear them up here.

While the F-27 continues inbound, the local one and local two controllers and the ground controller coordinate the shifting of all inbound and departing aircraft away from 25 Left. Runway 24 Right, used as little as possible due to noise abatement restrictions, takes up some of the load. The ground controller's job suddenly becomes more complex now because he'll be taxiing increased numbers of 24 Left and 24 Right arrivals from the north side of the field to their gates at the south terminals.

The last plane to touch down on 25 Left crosses 25 Right and continues to its gate.

Runway 25 Left now stands empty, ready to receive the F-27. In the air to the east, there are no landing lights yet visible along the runway's final approach course, but fire engines and ambulances, engines slowly ticking over, already line the right side of the runway.

Inbound pilots, expecting to land on one of the 25-runways, are surprised when told to plan on 24 Right. In the TRACON, immediately after the approach control team supervisor talked with the tower, controllers began diverting arriving traffic away from 25 Left. Other planes, departures from LAX, arrivals and departures from other area airports, and still other planes en route through the Los Angeles basin, are being directed away from the F-27's flight path toward LAX.

The west end of LAX's runways end practically at the beach, which is just a few hundred yards beyond the airport. While the F-27 continues inbound, the watch supervisor now telephones the Coast Guard's search and rescue coordinator at Venice Point, a few miles from the airport, and the harbormaster whose jurisdiction is just off the boundary of LAX. Next, he calls the beach lifeguard station and the local police station. If the F-27 should go into the water during an attempted go-around, or fall into any part of the city close to LAX, assistance will now be closer.

"What I can't understand," says the supervisor to no one in particular, "is why the F-twenty-seven says 'no equipment.' If the joker doesn't want equipment; he doesn't say anything about an emergency, right?"

Approach control calls; the F-27 is on twelve-mile final, 25 Left: "Do you want him now?"

"Yeah," answers the tower supervisor, "send him on over."

"Fairchild eight-four Bravo," advises the approach controller on his own radio frequency, *"twelve miles from end of runway, you're cleared to land two five Left, contact Los Angeles tower now, one one eight point nine. Good luck."*

"Tower one one eight point nine, eight-four Bravo."

Click-stopping his radio's frequency selector to the local one controller's frequency, 118.9, the F-27 makes its first contact with the tower.

"Los Angeles tower, Fairchild eight-four Bravo, twelve-mile final for two five Left."

"Roger, eight-four bravo," replies Ron Fraser, still working local one, *"very good, not in sight; continue for two five Left; you're cleared to land two five Left."*

"Eight-four Bravo."

Other planes land and depart LAX's three active runways. Three fire engines, two ambulances, the United States Coast Guard, the Los Angeles area harbor master, the lifeguard station on the beach, and perhaps a score of nearby police cars and city rescue units await the arrival of 84 Bravo.

"There he is! I got him," says Fraser to the other controllers in the cab.

"Fairchild eight-four Bravo, in sight now, you're looking good, runway two five Left, clear to land. Wind two five zero at five.

"Looking good eight-four Bravo; take all the time you need for your rollout; there's nobody behind you. No need to acknowledge, eight-four Bravo; wind's still two five zero at five."

As 84 Bravo touches down, the waiting fire engines and ambulances along the runway's right side shift into gear and keep pace with the F-27 as it slows, still moving down the runway.

"Eight-four Bravo," says Fraser, *"no need to acknowledge; right or left turn your choice clearing the runway. Stay with me."*

Apparently familiar with the airport, the F-27 turns left and slowly taxis toward the private aviation hangars on the south side of the field. Looking through their binoculars, controllers see that the plane's left engine is not turning, its propellor blades are feathered edge-on to reduce drag during the plane's single-engine flight and landing at LAX. The plane, followed by the fire engines and ambulances, taxis to Butler Aviation and shuts down its right engine.

"Hey, tower, thanks a lot," calls the F-27 pilot.

"No problem. Glad you made it."

The red rotating beacon at the top of the Fairchild's tail continues to flash for a moment, then goes dark as its pilot turns off the plane's master switch.

The tower supervisor picks up the phone and calls approach control, "O.K., you bastards," he jokes, "eight-four Bravo's down. No thanks to you."

"We figured you guys would get him killed for sure," answers the approach team supervisor.

As he hangs up the interphone to approach control, the tower supervisor picks up another handset and begins making calls to stand down the alert he'd set up to protect 84 Bravo.

Off duty for dinner now, Fraser stops by the ready-room to pick up Ted Merril for their walk to the airport employees' cafeteria.

"Hi, what's going on?" Merril asks by way of greeting.

"Nothing. Let's go to dinner," Fraser replies, pushing the elevator call button for the eleven-story ride down to the ground.

9   Ted Merril

It's no fun if you're a respected controller someplace else and when you get to a new facility you're made to feel like everybody's saying, 'Look dummy, now we're going to show you how to really control traffic.' You have to fight to maintain your individual style of controlling traffic. Your style is what helps you stay loose—which you have to do. Air traffic control is not a situation where you can choose what you want to deal with; you have to correct things quickly because it's fatal to let them continue.

TED MERRIL came to LAX tower from Palomar airport just outside Carlsbad, California, about eighty miles south of Los Angeles. Palomar's a small operation as airports go: 230,000 takeoffs and landings during 1977, one runway 4,700 feet long, and no air carrier operations. The transition from working mostly single-engine airplanes at Palomar to handling Boeing 747s along with having to work more than twice as fast, since Palomar's 615 operations a day were less than half the daily traffic at LAX, was, during his first few weeks at Los Angeles tower, almost more than Merril felt he was capable of.

But, before he was allowed to say *clear for takeoff* or *clear to land* to his first airplane at LAX, there were weeks of study at the tower's training facility. Merril attended no classes. All of his instruction was on a one-to-one basis and his instructor was not an instructor in the usual sense, but a GS-13 controller ($22,000 per year) whose main responsibility was to prepare Merril to handle his new job so that, from the first day he spoke into a microphone at LAX tower, he would be as ready as he could be to handle a split-second, 300-life emergency.

Weeks before he was allowed to work his first shift in the tower, Merril was required to memorize the following:

1. numbers, length, width, and weight-bearing capacity of every runway at LAX;

2. numbers, width, weight-bearing capacity, and starting and terminating points of every taxiway on the airport;

3. locations of the eight satellite passenger terminals, plus the names of the airlines which use each one, plus the gate numbers used by each airline which uses each terminal;

4. location of each airline's freight terminal in *cargo city* in the northeast corner of the airport; and

5. location of each airline's maintenance hangar—mostly in the south, central portion of the airport.

Merril was to draw and label maps of all this many times so that he could *quickly* clear a (perhaps emergency) landing onto a runway which was long enough and strong enough for the plane he was talking to; *quickly* route pilots (perhaps unfamiliar with the airport) to the terminal which their airline uses; quickly route cargoliners to freight terminals without delaying planeloads of passengers; and, *especially,* prevent at all times the situation of a plane on a taxiway blocking an exit from a runway where planes are landing or taking off. At other airports (and several times at LAX), such traffic jams have resulted in collisions on the ground which have taken lives.

Besides drawing and labeling maps of LAX, the new control-ler must memorize each of the thirteen communications frequencies and seven radio navigational aid frequencies assigned to LAX. There are three local control frequencies: 118.9 for runways 25 Left and Right (local one); 120.8 for runways 24 Left and Right (local two); and 119.8 for helicopters. There are two separate ground control frequencies; one clearance delivery frequency; three approach control frequencies; two departure control frequencies; one frequency each for the arrival and departure information recordings; and the universal emergency frequency, 121.5. The seven radio navigational frequencies have mostly to do with the airport's four instrument landing systems (ILS) which serve LAX's four jet runways. All of this must be memorized so that an airplane being handed off from one facility to another, or even from one runway to another, can quickly be told the appropriate communications and ILS frequencies; for this, too, happens under emergency conditions.

Finally, Merril must memorize the frequencies and locations of most radio navigational aids within a fifty-mile radius of LAX, plus the numbers and locations of all airways in the Los Angeles basin, plus the standard LAX arrival and departure routes, plus the direct line phone numbers to each of the other 22 FAA air traffic control facilities (mostly other airports) in the vicinity.

Only then, when he has committed all this, plus emergency procedures and special air traffic regulations to memory, is a new controller allowed to work traffic at LAX. And, once in the tower, he will have but limited time to memorize scores of aircraft reporting points and prominent landmarks displayed on the tower's radar.

At Palomar, Merril was one of the best, by many accounts *the* best, controller in the tower. He'd seen the notice of a vacancy at LAX tower on the bulletin board at Palomar and, along with perhaps fifty other controllers in the western United States, he'd filled out a lengthy form which included his Air Force air traffic training and experience six years earlier and mailed it, along with a letter, to Los Angeles. Merril and about twenty other controllers were interviewed for the job and, three weeks later, it was offered to him. Of all the experienced, fully-qualified controllers evaluated, Merril was judged the best. It was like going from an AAAA team to the major leagues.

"I used to sit up alone after getting off work nights," Merril says, "wondering if I did the best thing—coming to LAX—or if was I going to wash out there. 'God,' I used to think, 'if I don't make it at LAX, send me anyplace, but not back where I came from.' It was a terrible feeling.

"Advancement was what I came to LAX for. I had just made GS-11 ($16,500 per year) at Palomar and I wanted to improve myself faster in the FAA than I could by staying at Palomar. I'm twenty-nine and I want to use my youth while I have it going for me, so that, when I'm thirty-five and not as quick and sharp as you have to be to work traffic, I'll be able to move into management and have someplace to go.

"At LAX you don't wash out because of the traffic. You wash out because of the instructor. For example, I would do something like call an American flight 'United' and one of the instructors would say, 'You dummy!' And you have maybe three instructors, each with his own style; like on ground control, each one might have different routes and taxiways he likes to use to move planes around the airport. Your way isn't any worse than their way, but each one thinks his way is a little bit faster and they'll practically put a stopwatch on you and say, 'O.K., you delayed that United a minute because you went your way, but he wouldn't have been delayed that minute if he'd gone my way.' After a while it gets to you and you end up concentrating more on what your instructor's going to say than on what you're doing. Just today one of the instructors was standing right behind me nipping at my back and after a while his standing there was psyching me out so bad I was doing a rotten job. He was there all the time bugging me, taking away my concentration.

"On the other hand, I don't think there's any one way to train people. Ron Fraser stands very close to you, and he makes you think—always asking you what you think you should do next, training you to think ahead. Steve Wilkins is entirely different; he gets about as far away from you as the length of the cord on his headset will let him and still be able to see the traffic you're working. You try to do your best for him just to prove you can really do it without him standing right there.

"Some guys' styles of controlling traffic are something to see! There's no way in the world those pilots down there can see us up in the tower, but, the way some guys act, you'd never know it. There's one guy, who, whenever he clears somebody to take off, takes his arm and swings it like he was waving the starting flag at the Indianapolis 500. Then there are others who are 'pointers'; while they're talking to the pilot they're pointing out everything he's supposed to do: 'follow the American ahead,' and they point to it; 'turn left, taxiway 47 to the gate,' and they're showing him which direction is left, and pointing to the taxiway he's supposed to follow. Or, when they tell a plane that's taxiing to stop and hold its position, they'll hold up their hand like a traffic cop. Other guys will mimic the pilots' accents. Delta has a lot of southern pilots and one of the guys answered one of them with this broad put-on southern accent he can do, and the Delta pilot caught it, came right back, and said, 'Are you mockin' me, boy?'

"We've got one woman controller in the tower, Pat Hammond. We'll be pumping traffic with no let up—one runway closed, some taxiways closed, and the airport in a real mess—and she'll keep the traffic moving when there is no way anyone could do it. There were times when she had to tell pilots, 'O.K., everybody stop talking, I can only hear one at a time,' and then she'll correct whatever's gone wrong. After she's done something impossible she doesn't come on and say, 'There! See what I've done.' She knows she's damn good and that everybody in the cab knows she's damn good and they respect her for it. Many times she'll get you out of trouble and, unless you're very aware of how she's working the traffic, you won't even have time to know you were in trouble. She's that smooth. She's never been my instructor, but I've learned a lot from her.

"I've been in the tower a couple of months now and I'm beginning to teach myself. I'm slowly working traffic more my own style, trying it my way. If my way's slower I'll see why, mark that way off, and try another way. I don't get tense. I don't feel tense, but when I drive the freeway I get upset and holler and scream at the traffic. I try not to bring it home. I get uptight when my wife asks me questions about work. I tell her, 'I don't have the patience to explain it all to you; I had it all day!' She doesn't need to know about it.

"Comfortable with it? You're never comfortable. You get to the point where you feel confident, but you're never comfortable. I don't think anybody is."

10 Collision on Runway 27 Left

Controllers in the [Chicago O'Hare] tower saw the flash through the heavy fog, but couldn't see the DC-9 burning on the runway. The control tower supervisor sounded the crash alarm when pilots reported something burning on the runway. . . . Ten passengers were killed, and eleven passengers and crew were injured.

—FAA Spokesman

The National Transportation Safety Board determines that the probable cause of this accident was the failure of the air traffic control system to insure separation of aircraft during a period of restricted visibility. . . . The [ground] controller omitted a critical word which made his transmission . . . ambiguous.

—NTSB Final Report

ON THE afternoon of the fatal collision on Chicago O'Hare's runway 27 Left, the airport's tower was being worked by two local controllers, each handling a different runway, one ground controller, a clearance delivery controller, a flight (plan) data controller, and a supervisor. It has been many years since any but the smallest airports having a control tower have been operated with only one controller on duty at a time. Almost every major air terminal functions today with six or seven controllers sequencing the movement of planes landing and taking off, moving to and from the runways and terminal gates, and receiving flight plan clearances. Even relatively minor airports served by airlines usually split control tower duties between a local controller who talks to pilots landing and taking off and a ground controller who communicates with planes moving on the terminal ramp and taxiways. The busier the airport, the greater chance there is for a breakdown in communications between controllers and pilots, and between controllers themselves.

Unlike Los Angeles International's four parallel runways, the runways at Chicago O'Hare form two separate airports, each having the traditional pattern of three runways in a more or less equilateral triangle. O'Hare's control tower and passenger terminals are located between the separate "airports," which are situated to provide three sets of parallel runways. As at other airports, O'Hare's runways are numbered according to the magnetic heading of an aircraft using the runway. Runway 27, for example, is 270 degrees due west. Runway 36 would be due north; runway 18, due south, and so on. Since a runway can be used in either direction, it has two numbers. Runway 14, 140 degrees, becomes runway 32, 320 degrees, when used in the opposite direction. Each of O'Hare's two airports has a runway 14/32, and they are differentiated in communications to pilots by calling them 14 Left or Right, and 32 Left or Right.

The weather most of the day had been unpleasant for everyone. A thick overcast made the short, mid-December day depressingly dark, and heavy fog restricted visibility. Auto drivers kept their headlights turned on most of the day, and Chicago police reported an unusually high number of rush hour accidents along the city's Lake Shore Drive. On the ground, temperatures during the day hovered near freezing, and the humidity was never far from 100 percent. Aloft, inside the overcast, the temperature was

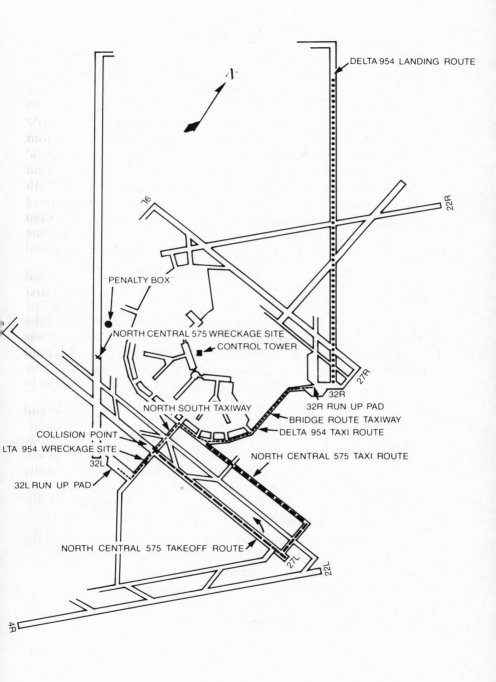

DELTA 954 LANDING ROUTE

22R

76

PENALTY BOX

NORTH CENTRAL 575 WRECKAGE SITE

CONTROL TOWER

27R

32R

32R RUN UP PAD

NORTH SOUTH TAXIWAY

BRIDGE ROUTE TAXIWAY

DELTA 954 TAXI ROUTE

COLLISION POINT

LTA 954 WRECKAGE SITE

NORTH CENTRAL 575 TAXI ROUTE

32L

32L RUN UP PAD

NORTH CENTRAL 575 TAKEOFF ROUTE

27L

22L

4R

well below 32 degrees. As arriving pilots descended into the clouds, they turned on deicing equipment, windshield defrosters, and other heaters to make sure that external sensors for airspeed and altitude instruments remained free of ice. The ceiling, when the four-engine Delta Air Lines jet touched down on runway 14 Left at 5:54 P.M., was a ragged 200 feet, and visibility was little more than a quarter-mile. It was impossible to see the plane from the 198-foot tower, and the ground controller was using pilots' position reports and surface radar (which suffered from blind spots) to move traffic on the terminal ramp and taxiways. Both pilots and controllers were relying on their intimate knowledge of the airport layout to manage movement on the ground. More than once in such weather, pilots who were new to the field had become lost and trucks had to be sent out to guide them to the terminal or departure runway.

Weather delays during the day had crowded the terminal gates and ramp with late departures and arrivals. When the first officer of Delta 954 radioed his company dispatcher as the plane cleared the runway, he was told to go to a holding pad, called the penalty box, to await gate assignment. Since the penalty box was located on the ramp close to runway 14 Right, the plane would have to taxi from the downwind end of 14 Left (32 Right) by following a taxiway around the perimeter of the terminal ramp to the "other" airport.

Part of the taxiway between the downwind end of 14 Left and the terminal is actually a bridge, which forms a convenient reporting point for pilots. *Inside the bridge* means between the bridge and the terminal. *Outside the bridge* means the plane is between the bridge and the runway. The bridge is a useful and commonly used reporting point, especially during poor visibility.

Contacting the ground controller after speaking with his dispatcher, the plane's first officer reported, "Delta nine fifty-four is with you inside the bridge and we gotta go to the "penalty box."

The controller replied, "O.K., if you can just pull over to the [runway] three-two [run-up] pad."

"O.K., we'll do it," the first officer replied.

In the cockpit, as the pilot partially advanced his throttles and the high-pitched whine of four jet engines increased, the airliner began to roll through dense fog toward the fiery collision which would soon take the lives of ten passengers.

Though tapes later played by investigators recorded the phrase, the ground controller failed to hear Delta's first officer report his position as inside the bridge. Believing he had instructed the pilot to stay on the east side of the field, holding on the runway-32-Right (downwind end of 14 Left) run-up pad, he had sent the plane toward the run-up pad for runway 32 Left on the west side of the airport, a path that took the plane across runway 27 Left, then being used for takeoffs.

Seven minutes before Delta 954 started moving toward the runway-32-Left run-up pad, the ground controller had cleared North Central Airlines flight 575, a DC-9, to taxi to runway 27 Left for departure.

Less than two minutes after Delta 954 began to taxi toward the runway-32-Left run-up pad, the local controller cleared North Central 575 into takeoff position on 27 Left and advised the pilot that visibility was one-quarter mile.

Twenty-six seconds later, the local controller cleared North Central 575 for takeoff.

The first officer was making the takeoff. As he applied full power and guided the plane down the runway, the captain called out the plane's increasing airspeed.

At the moment the plane reached the speed at which it was ready to fly, the captain saw another aircraft ahead on the runway.

At full power, and with the profile of the aircraft ahead of them rapidly looming larger in their windshield, the two North Central pilots hauled back on their DC-9's controls in an attempt to gain altitude to clear the four-engine Delta Convair. The DC-9 staggered into the air and for a few seconds the pilots' attempt to avert disaster seemed successful. Then the DC-9 slammed into the Convair, depressing its aft main cabin to within thirty-eight inches of the floor and making numerous other depressions in the top of the larger plane's cabin. The DC-9 captain, knowing the aircraft could not maintain flight, took over and flew the plane back to the runway.

When the plane came to a stop the captain quickly entered the cabin through the cockpit door and called to the passengers to come forward. He then went outside through the main entry door. From a position outside the aircraft, he assisted passengers down to the ground. With the aircraft already on fire, he re-entered the cabin and assisted other passengers through the main entry door. Nine of the ten fatally injured passengers failed to escape the aircraft. Post-accident examinations indicated that they had received no traumatic injuries, but succumbed instead to the effects of smoke inhalation, or burns, or both.

The minute the collision occured, the captain of the Delta Convair stopped the aircraft and shut down all four engines. All four main exits were opened and emergency slides were deployed and inflated. The plane was evacuated in approximately five minutes. Two passengers received minor injuries. There were eighty-six passengers and seven crew members aboard the Convair 880; there were forty-one passengers and four crewmembers aboard the DC-9.

Although a contributing factor to the accident was the ground controller's failure to hear, or comprehend, the Delta pilot's position report inside the bridge, the primary probable cause of the accident was the ground controller's ommission of *one word* from his instructions to the Delta pilot. If, when the Delta pilot reported, *"Delta nine five-four is with you inside the bridge and we gotta go to the penalty box,"* the ground controller had replied *"O.K., if you can just go over to the three two Left pad,"* the collision would not have occured.

One word, the word "Left," had been inadvertantly omitted —and was responsible for the loss of ten lives.

Five years later, on March 30, 1977, in the Canary Islands, a similar collision between a Boeing 747 taking off in the fog and another 747 taxiing on the runway, claimed the lives of more than

550 passengers and crew. The cause was a "simple" misunderstanding between an air traffic controller and the crew of a plane on the ground.

It is a problem technology can't solve. It could happen again —any time.

11   Los Angeles Ground

The other day a 747 Pan Am Clipper 5 that goes to Honolulu taxied from the gate with nobody in it. The pilot said, 'Ground control, this is Clipper 5 at the gate, we'd like to pushback,' and the ground controller said, 'Pushback approved, taxi to runway 24 Left.' They pulled that airplane out of the gate and started toward the runway and the Clipper said, 'Ground control, Clipper 5, we'd like to hold right here,' and the ground controller asked, 'You got a problem?,' and Clipper 5 said, 'Yeah, we forgot the passengers.'

AT ANY moment, there are close to seventy-five airliners on the ground at LAX. Thirty-six airlines (from Aerolineas Argentinas to Western Airlines) regularly serve the airport, as do three commuter airlines with frequent flights serving cities within California. Twenty-four additional airlines, including Aeroflot, Alaska Airlines, Pacific Western, Polish Airlines, Transavia Airways, and Yugoslav Airways also land at, take off from, and taxi on the surface of Los Angeles International. There are also 115,000 private-plane landings and takeoffs each year, which

89

averages out to just over 400 non-airline operations each day.

The main passenger terminals, along with automobile parking lots and restaurants, bars and cocktail lounges, banks, barber shops, newsstands, and car rental counters which make up the passenger service areas are located between the two south runways (25 Left and Right) and the two north runways (24 Left and Right).

In addition, there are eighty-four gates in almost constant use at the eight satellite terminals between the two south and two north runways. West of the main satellite terminals, also between the north and south runways, are major maintenance facilities operated by American Airlines, Continental, and TWA. Due east of the satellites, still between the north and south runways, is *Cargo City* used by Flying Tiger, Airlift International, and the cargoliners of United, Pan American, and other foreign and domestic air carriers.

Of the seventy-five or so airliners on the field at any one time, at least fifty are moving, are just about to move, or have just stopped moving at a passenger terminal, cargo area, or maintenance ramp. Even on one of LAX's "slow" days, there are likely to be fifty takeoffs and landings each hour.

What all this adds up to for the ground controller is a lot of work: for, at LAX, not one jet airliner starts its engines at the gate, is pushed back from its terminal, taxis to a runway, moves from its landing runway to the gate, or taxis, or is towed to or from a maintenance hangar or cargo terminal without approval from the LAX ground controller.

There are two taxiways, 47 and 49, which cross the field just west of the terminals to join the two 25 runways with the two 24 runways. There's a long taxiway, taxiway Uniform, which runs parallel to runway 24 Left, between it and the two north terminals. There's another long taxiway between runway 25 Right and the south terminals called taxiway Juliet. There's one more fairly long taxiway called Foxtrot, occasionally also serving as a runway for small planes, which is to the left of runway 25 Left. That's it.

Except for a few high speed turnoffs (short taxiways angled to allow landing planes to clear the runway without fully slowing) and several taxiways connecting 25 Left with 25 Right and 24 Left with 24 Right, the ground controller must move all departing and landing traffic, plus whatever else has to get from one point to another on the airport surface, using these limited facilities. Unlike a number of other airports, LAX has no circumferential taxiway circling the runways and terminal buildings.

It's Monday morning and Pat Hammond, the tower's only female controller, is preparing to rotate to ground control from another position. Her tall, slender figure, blue eyes, long brown hair, and vivacious face don't seem out-of-place here, but she wouldn't look out-of-place on the pages of *Harper's Bazaar*—or driving a racing car—either. For almost an hour, the air traffic information service (ATIS) recording, broadcast for arriving and departing pilots, has been repeating bad news: "Los Angeles information *X-ray,* 15:42 weather: measured ceiling two eight hundred overcast, visibility twelve, temperature six one, dew point five four, wind one hundred degrees at eight, altimeter two nine point nine eight. Notice to airmen: taxiway four seven closed. All aircraft advise the tower when number one for departure. Departing aircraft remain below the two five hundred-floor of the VFR corridor until west of the shoreline. Advise ground control of first vector fix and that you have information *X-ray.* "

Its the second sentence of the ATIS recording which contain's Pat's bad news: taxiway 47, one of the two taxiways connecting the south side of the field with the north, along with its short-access runways to the commuter terminal, is closed for repairs. She'll have only one taxiway, number 49 (too narrow for planes going in opposite directions to pass each other) available for use in moving traffic north and south. As she plugs in her headset to observe the position for several minutes before taking over, there are already twelve jumbos (747s, wide-body DC-10s, and L-1011s) lined up on taxiway Uniform, for departure on runways 24 Left and 24 Right. If they don't take off soon, the growing line of jumbos will block Pat Hammond's one "crosstown" taxiway (49), forcing her to hold additional jumbos at their gates and backing up still more jumbos (now landing on both 25 Left and 24 Right) on other taxiways south and north of the terminals.

At this moment, a 747, United Airlines flight 100 to Chicago, sits motionless in takeoff position on runway 24 Left. The plane isn't under Pat's jurisdiction. When the pilot had reported number one for takeoff, the flight had been turned over to the local two controller and the pilot changed from the ground control frequency to 120.8, the tower [local two] frequency for runways 24 Left and 24 Right.

"United one hundred," repeats the local two controller in his third attempt to contact the 747, *"Los Angeles tower, I say again, clear for immediate takeoff.*

"United one hundred, one, two, three, four, five; five, four, three, two, one. How do you read the tower?"

"Try him, Pat," asks Jerry Feldman the local two man, "maybe he's gone back to ground."

"United one hundred," asks Pat Hammond, *"Los Angeles ground, how do you read?"*

On the runway United 100 remains unresponsive. Twelve miles east of the airport another jumbo, United 185, a DC-10 from Chicago, has been told to continue its approach for landing on 24 Left. If United 100 doesn't respond immediately, United 185 may have to be sent around and somehow re-sequenced into the almost solid lines of arriving aircraft.

"He's not answering, Jerry," Pat tells the local two controller. "He's probably got a stuck microphone switch and his transmitter's on so he can't hear a thing. We may have to send a car out there if he doesn't realize what's happening."

"Los Angeles tower, United one hundred," the 747 finally calls from runway 24 Left.

"United one hundred, maintain your position, company traffic on final for two four Left," the local two tells the 747 pilot.

A split second later, the local two controller asks the now very close United DC-10, *"United one eighty-five, on final for two four Left, can you change to two four Right?"*

"United one eighty-five, that's affirmative."

"O.K., clear to land two four Right, wind one hundred at eight."

"O.K. United one eighty-five's clear for two four Right," responds the pilot of the landing DC-10 as he changes his heading slightly to the right, making the small adjustment necessary to align his airplane with his new runway assignment.

As soon as United 185 confirms that he'll be able to change his landing from 24 Left to 24 Right, the local two controller clears United 100 for takeoff. The entire incident takes place in less than two minutes.

"O.K., gentlemen," Pat Hammond advises the other jumbos monitoring ground control, *"we're back in business again."* Microphone switches don't stick every day, especially without a plane's crew realizing it, but it's happened to every pilot in the waiting line often enough so that he understands, and grudgingly accepts, the delay which has just taken place.

With United 100 out of the way, the long line of soon-to-depart jumbos on taxiway Uniform slowly moves forward as, one by one, the local two controller clears them for takeoff. Pat Hammond begins clearing other jumbos from their gates to 24 Left. She also begins clearing other recently landed planes to gates now being vacated by the airliners she'd been forced to hold there.

"TWA four sixty," she tells a jumbo which she'd been holding at gate 32, *"pushback approved for two four. Taxi four nine for Uniform. Taxiway four seven is closed."*

"United one eighty-five," she now tells the DC-10 which has just landed on 24 Right, *"hold short of taxiway four nine; northbound traffic on four nine for Uniform. Taxiway four seven's closed."*

"Hold short of four nine, United one eighty-five."

A few moments later, as TWA 460 clears taxiway 49 and turns right on Uniform, Pat tells the waiting DC-10:

"United one eighty-five, taxi four nine now to the gate."

"United ninety-eight, ready for pushback, gate eight two, Seal Beach with X-ray."

"*United ninety-eight,*" advises Pat, "*push back for two five.*"

"Hughesair nine eighty-three," calls a landing flight as it departs 25 Right, "goin' [gate] to sixteen."

"*Hughesair nine eighty-three, taxi to the gate.*"

"Ground control, this is Mexicana nine fifteen, gate five six, are we clear to push back?" asks the Spanish accented voice of a 727 bound for Guadalajara.

"*Mexicana nine fifteen,*" responds Pat clearly and slowly for the foreign pilot, "*that's affirmative you are cleared to push back from the gate. Taxi to runway two five Right.*"

"Royer," answers Mexicana 915.

"United three eighty, taxi outta seven nine, to Gorman with X-ray."

"*United three eighty, taxi to two five Right, follow the PSA just passing southbound on your right.*"

"Two five Right, behind the PSA, for United three eighty."

"LA Ground, PSA one sixty-three's ready for pushback. Ventura."

"*PSA one sixty-three, ground, push back for two five.*"

Close coordination between Pat and the local one and local two controllers sometimes allows her to inform a plane taxiing for departure exactly which runway will be assigned for takeoff. But, often during a departure rush, neither local controller can be sure which of his runways he'll use; so the ground controller is only able to say, "Taxi for 25," or, "Taxi for 24." The local controller then makes the final runway assignment—left or right runway— just before the plane takes off.

"Delta eleven ninety-seven's clear two four."

"*Delta eleven ninety-seven, taxi four nine to the gate. Taxiway four seven's closed.*"

"Delta eleven ninety-seven, roger, four nine to the gate."

"Ground, TWA twenty-two's ready for pushback outta three seven with X-ray."

"*TWA twenty-two, ground, push back for two four, hold short of four nine, southbound Delta traffic. Taxiway four seven closed. After the Delta's clear, taxi four nine for Uniform.*"

"TWA twenty-two, short for Delta, then four nine to Uniform."

"Continental seven thirty-seven, clear two five to the gate."

"Continental seven thirty-seven, make right turn south of the American satellite, then go east of American to the gate.

"Continental seven thirty-seven, you copy?"

"We got it, Continental seven thirty-seven."

"Golden Airwest eight thirty-five, ready to taxi with the numbers."

"Golden Airwest eight thirty-five was it?"

"That's affirm."

"O.K., eight thirty-five, hold in the ramp area, I'll get back to you."

"American twelve's clear two five for gate four six."

"American twelve, taxi to the gate."

"Golden Airwest from commuter terminal to the barn."

"Golden Airwest, roger, hold in the ramp area, you'll follow your company. Be ready to taxi."

LAX's commuter terminal fronts on closed taxiway 47; so, today, only short auxiliary taxiways which normally connect 47 and 49 with each other, and with the ramp areas, are available to move commuter flights to and from their terminal between the north and south satellites.

"American two is ready for pushback."

"American two, taxi to two four Left."

"Now, Golden Airwest eight thirty-five, follow the American DC-ten that's on the ramp west of the satellites—and, Golden Airwest two hundred, you follow your company."

"Golden Airwest eight thirty-five."

"Golden Airwest two hundred."

As they often are because of personnel shortages and overtime limitations, ground control one (the 25 runways and south terminals) and ground control two (the 24 runways and north terminals) are combined this morning, and Pat Hammond is solely responsible for both positions. There is less danger of a fatal accident with this combination, than there would be with a combination of local one and local two, which control aircraft in flight.

As Pat continues working the combined ground control positions, mainly from the number one position by the watch supervisor's desk, the supervisor's phone rings:

"Los Angeles tower, Lampton," says Vinnie Lampton, serving as temporary supervisor for this watch.

"Yes ma'am; no ma'am; we really haven't; we couldn't even if we wanted to and, believe me, we don't; no ma'am, they haven't; no one could do that anyhow because the planes have to fly a very straight approach. Yes ma'am, I will. Good-bye. You take care now."

Without taking her eyes from the traffic she's working to check Vinnie's expression, Pat knows who the caller was: a lady who lives near the airport along the approach course for the 24 runways who's convinced the FAA has curved the 24 approach path over her house so that landing planes will avoid disturbing the guests at the Ramada Inn on Century Boulevard near her home. She calls three or four times a week and the conversation is always the same. The crew would start worrying about her if she stopped phoning.

While working ground control, Pat Hammond will have directed and coordinated the movements of more than twice the number of aircraft worked by both local controllers; because, in addition to landing and departing airliners, she will also have sequenced the movements of planes to and from maintenance hangars, the satellites, and freight terminals.

There was one aborted takeoff this morning. As a Pan Am 747 was just about to attain flying speed departing 24 Left, the airplane abruptly slowed on the runway. Smoke billowed from its wheels as the plane made every effort to stop before rolling off the end. As the 747 turned off the runway, Pat asked if emergency equipment was required and whether any other assistance was needed. "Oh, no," replied the co-pilot, "the captain just forgot to lock his seat in place. When we applied full power he was holding the wheel and his seat slid all the way back."

12   Pat Hammond

When you get certified on ground control it's the most fun position to work. Everyone in the tower says 'Hey, I want some time on ground control!,' and they mean it. Everybody likes to work the morning departure rush because you have to do everything right and you've always got to be ready to handle anything. You do a lot of wheelin' and dealin', and when you do a good job you feel great.

"I'VE BEEN a   controller—wow!—fourteen years now. I went into the Navy fresh out of high school and picked this occupation because of a picture I saw in a Navy occupational handbook—a WAVE in a tower with a microphone talking to airplanes. Before that, my only job was in a laundry. I shook out clothes that came out of the washers and got them set on a long table so they could be run through the mangle; then, next, I was up at the mangle running the clothes through; then, I was down at the end of the line catching them when they came out. I finished high school while I still had that job and was supposed to get married, but it didn't work out. I didn't want to

97

get married so I joined the Navy.

"When I got out of Air Controllerman School I worked at Pensacola, then came out to Alameda Naval Air Station here in California. When I got out of the Navy, the FAA was the natural place to go.

"I have to admit, I think I've been on the receiving end of some prejudice against women. My first FAA tower assignment was at Stockton about sixty miles east of San Francisco. We were a reliever airport for San Francisco and one day we got a call that we could expect some extra arrivals because the weather had gone down at San Francisco and they'd had to close the airport.

"I was working local control and so right away this old-timer came over to where I was working and said he'd better take over on local because we were going to be busy. So I thought, 'What the hell, here we are with beautiful weather, I can do it, but I said, 'O.K.' I told this guy the only thing I had was a single-engine Cessna 210 five miles out and that I'd cleared him to land. Then I went over to work ground control.

"Well, a minute later I looked up and here comes this Cessna, but his gear wasn't down. So I said, 'Hey, Jim, that Cessna's gear isn't down,' and he said 'What?', and I told him again, "That Cessna's gear isn't down.' The Cessna kept coming and Jim didn't do anything.

"So again I told him, 'Jim, you'd better tell that Cessna his gear isn't down,' and he said, 'He doesn't have a retractable gear.' By this time he'd picked up the binoculars and there the Cessna was, landed with his wheels up.

"I was bitter because he'd taken me off the position in the first place, so when the chief asked me about the incident I told him exactly how I felt. That was the first time I was aware that maybe the FAA would think of me as a different kind of controller because I was female and not have any confidence in my opinion being worth anything because I was a woman.

"At LAX you don't find attitudes like that. Everybody here is super-competent and we work very closely together. In many ways controllers who work together know each other better than they know their husbands and wives. You have to intuitively know how the other person's going to react to an emergency situation so you can flow with it instead of against it—and that often has to happen without words. So you're sub-consciously sort of reaching for contact on some emotional level and you become very sensitive. I think policemen working as partners often do that.

"Working ground control requires very close teamwork with local one—keeping those high speed turnoffs clear so that one of them isn't blocked when landing traffic has to clear the runway. Getting airplanes from the gate to their departure runway isn't just, 'everybody to 25 Right except the wide-bodies.' You really have to listen for their departure route so you can try and send most of the north and east departures to the north complex (24 Left and Right) and most of the west and south departures to the south complex (25 Left and Right). You can't always do that because the local one or local two controller might have too much landing traffic to take any departures for a while. So you've got to be a good local controller yourself, and you've got to constantly be aware of each local controller's situation so that you don't have to all the time be asking them, 'Can you take this one?' or 'Can you take that one?' Questions are the last thing they need. You have to coordinate the flow without very much talking.

"Last time I was working ground, the local one controller had an inbound American jet cleared to land 25 Right and when he looked up at the American it was lined up for 25 Left. There was Hughesair jet in position on 25 Left cleared for takeoff and rolling, but it wasn't rolling soon enough so that the American would be able to land; so he had to send the American around. The local one man just can't be distracted by questions. If he'd looked at me for a second, he might have missed that American landing on the wrong runway and we could have had a disaster.

"Training new people is part of every controller's job. Not everybody likes it. In fact controllers' on-the-job training responsibilities are a sore point between the FAA and our union, PATCO, the Professional Air Traffic Controllers Organization. Some of the guys in the tower hate doing training, and some of us like it; so it pretty much evens out. It's really not safe to assign anyone to full-time instructing in a tower. Whoever's doing the teaching has to be very, very familiar with working the position he's instructing on, because, as instructor, you're the back-up if the trainee goofs. Your headset is plugged in on the position and you have to be able to make the right moves fast if something suddenly goes wrong.

"You feel a lot more stress training someone than you do when you're working the position yourself. With a trainee, you have to let things go a bit further than you normally would just to see if he'll recognize the situation and correct it. And you're always aware that you're distracted when you're training someone and that you might miss something that you'd otherwise catch. Instructing a trainee on ground you have to have a nice chalk-talk first and explain the standard instrument departures 90 percent of the airplanes use. After I've told and shown a trainee everything I can, I'll let him get in there and work the position and stumble through for a little while and then I'll say, 'O.K., sit back and take it easy for a minute,' and then I'll work it and show him how to do something. Then we'll go downstairs and we'll have another chalk-talk and I'll explain something I did or show him why he was wrong on something he did.

"One thing that helps when you're training people is that anyone who comes here was a fully-rated controller someplace else; so you're not exactly teaching Air Traffic Control 101. But even a new assistant tower chief—watch supervisor—coming here from another facility has to start as a trainee and qualify on every position before he can take over his new job.

"Personally, I don't ever see myself going into management. You have too many books and rules to follow and it's so bureaucratic you can't do anything. Until recently I haven't thought about what's going to happen when I lose it, but I'm thirty-two and I have to realize that I'm going to lose it some day. And I have nightmares now. In the last one I was working as watch supervisor only I wasn't in the tower. I was on the airport somewhere with these two controllers who worked the last mid-watch with me, and

I looked up and saw this PSA climbing so steep I knew he was going to stall and I turned to the other two guys and said, 'Hey, that's not going to work at all!' and the other guys are saying, 'Yeah, yeah, no problem,' and then I'm seeing the PSA go down and crash. We started running to get back to the tower, but there was a high, chain-link fence and the gate was locked and we all looked frantically in our pockets, but no one had the key; so we couldn't get in.

"I've been involved in some real close calls and afterward my confidence just went 'crash.' I was so nervous, and when I got on local I felt I was being watched—that people were saying, 'Hey, she screwed up, let's keep an eye on her.'

"They probably knew what I was going through and that I was going to be shaky. So what I did was to try and work traffic at my own pace, but it's really clumsy to try and slow traffic down because the normal thing is to get in there and wheel and deal and keep 'em moving. You don't have any control over the pace. If you try and slow things down, pretty soon traffic's backed up all the way to Las Vegas. You're a captive of the system.

"Unlike the way it is with the married controllers, my social life hasn't become a captive of the system. I think it's more my being the *kind* of person who's a controller, rather than the fact that I am a controller, which affects my social life. I almost got married when I got out of high school, but joined the Navy instead. Then there was one time at Alameda when I almost got married, but we just drifted apart. I don't think he's married to this day. Then I almost got married when I worked for a while at Hayward (California) tower. I thought, 'Hey, this guy is really super,' then I decided I didn't like my job and wham, bam, I was gone. I've met guys who'd say to me, 'Who's going to want to marry you, when here you are with a nice apartment and driving around in a new car?' I think the only reason that would bother anyone is if they're not confident of themselves and need someone to make them feel superior—and I'm not going to want that kind of relationship anyway.

"I guess I put my career above everything else. I got some

college in the Navy and I'm starting again part-time. I think I'd like to go to law school. But you know what else I'd really like to do? I think I'd like to own a bar—be a bartender. I really would."

13 Turn Clipper Five-Now!

It's not a perfect system, and there's no system in the world that's perfect. They tell the public that, 'the system is as safe as it can be,' but how safe is that? When you have the human element there are always going to be errors.

THE TRAFFIC at LAX is heavy, but no more than usual for a busy period of the day. The sky is overcast, fairly uncommon for summer, with the base of the cloud layer just below 2,000 feet and the tops between 3,000 and 4,000. The ATIS weather broadcast is reporting seven miles visibility, with the wind from about 230 degrees at ten knots. The presence of a cloud layer is usually little more than a nuisance to departing pilots. The cockpit windows seem briefly to be painted an opaque white, as the plane quickly passes through the clouds. At the moment, air traffic is heavy north and southbound along the shoreline just west of LAX, and air traffic controllers are playing it safe by restricting departures to 2,000 feet until they are well west of the north-south traffic; so there will be no chance of planes on intersecting flight paths meeting in mid-air.

For the past forty-five minutes the local two controller working runways 24 Right and Left has been departing an almost solid
string of 747s, giant DC-10s, and L-1011s: one every three minutes
except when he has to briefly use 24 Left for occasional landings.
Since 24 Left is his "inboard" runway, he uses it as much as
possible for takeoffs. Landings, especially jumbo landings, are
quieter than takeoffs; so he assigns landings to 24 Right, which is
closer to the airport boundary and the nearby housing develop-
ments north of the airport. Most of his departures have been north
or northeast bound so there's been little need to coordinate with
the local one controller working runways 25 Right and Left on the
airport's south side. Any southbound departure from either of the
24 runways requires coordination with the local one controller.
The controllers must make sure that any plane turning left (south)
across the 25 runways' departure course won't collide with a plane
departing 25 Right or 25 Left. Usually, the local one controller has
only to hold his next departure on the ground until any plane
turning south from either of the 24s is well clear of the 25 runways'
departure course.

The local one controller's activity is also routine. PSA 190
from Sacramento, a few minutes late because of the weather, has
just cleared 25 Right after landing, and now taxis to its terminal.
American 533, which landed on 25 Right soon after PSA 190
cleared the runway, is now turning off the west end of the runway
to taxi the short distance to its terminal—last in the row of five
which serve the south runway complex.

American 21, a wide-body DC-10 non-stop from New York,
reports over Lima:

"Los Angeles, American twenty-one, Lima for two five Left."

*"American twenty-one, Los Angeles, runway two five Left, clear
to land. Wind two three zero at ten."*

"American twenty-one."

Soon American 12, another DC-10, now being pushed back
from its gate, will be taxiing for takeoff—on 25 Left, if possible,
since it's a southbound departure headed for San Diego.

Close to the east end of 25 Right, a PSA 727, flight 163 for

San Jose, and Western 983, a Boeing 720 bound for San Francisco, wait their turns for takeoff. They're both northbound flights; so their crossover of the 24 runways' departure course will have to be closely coordinated with the local two controller.

"American twenty-one, second high speed turnoff, clear to cross two five Right, ground point seven five clearing."

"American twenty-one's clear to cross the right, ground point seven five."

"PSA one sixty-three, two five Right," says the local one controller as American 21 continues west on the taxiway toward its terminal after crossing 25 Right, *"clear for takeoff. Wind two three zero at ten."*

The local two controller will hold his next departure until the tower radar shows that PSA 163 is well clear of his runways' departure course.

On the run-up pad for 24 Left, Clipper five, a Pan Am 747 bound for Honolulu, awaits takeoff clearance.

On the south side of the airport, a corporate twin-engine turboprop Aero Commander, N 8637 Tango, taxis from the ramp toward 25 Left, its departure runway.

At this moment in the TRACON, the departure one controller, a trainee working southbound departures, is distracted by the pilot of Beechcraft N 5954 Delta, who has just called for clearance into the TCA. The situation, normally not a problem, has become of immediate and compelling concern to the trainee and his instructor because the position given by the Beechcraft, 60 degrees from the LAX radio navigational station, is precisely on the approach course for more than a dozen airliners descending in close-spaced single file for landing at LAX.

With inbound airliners popping out of the bottom of the overcast close to the Beechcraft's possible position and altitude, 60 degrees from LAX, a mid-air collision could happen at any moment.

"Beechcraft fifty-four Delta," asks the trainee controller attempting to quickly verify the small plane's position, *"You say you departed Long Beach and you're en route to Santa Monica at one*

eight hundred feet on the Los Angeles VOR six zero degree radial?"

"That's affirmative, fifty-four Delta."

"Fifty-four Delta, squawk seven two two five (on your transponder) *and ident."*

"Fifty-four Delta, ident seven two two five."

Scanning his radarscope along a 60 degree line from LAX, the controller watches for the blinking data block which should show 54 Delta's position. Nothing; the data block, blinking to show that the plane's pilot has pushed the *ident* feature of his transponder, fails to appear.

"Fifty-four Delta," now asks the controller, *"say your distance from the Los Angeles International VOR."*

"Negative DME (distance measuring equipment)," responds the pilot.

As the departure controller and his instructor continue their concentration on Beechcraft 54 Delta, the controller working local one in the tower clears Aero Commander 8637 Tango for takeoff.

"Aero Commander eighty-six thirty-seven Tango, two five Left, clear for takeoff; maintain two thousand; expect higher. Wind two three zero at ten."

"Commander thirty-seven Tango, maintain two."

"Departure," says the local one controller, pushing the button which connects his headset with departure control, *"Aero Commander eighty-six thirty-seven Tango's off two five Left."*

At nearly that same instant, the local two controller, who moments before had ordered Clipper five into position on 24 Left, clears the 747 for takeoff.

"Clipper five, two four Left, clear for takeoff; maintain two-thousand; expect higher from departure. Wind two three zero at ten."

"Clipper five, clear for takeoff; maintain two," responds the Pan Am pilot as his plane begins to move down the runway.

The departure controller and his instructor, still intensely occupied with the Beechcraft reported on the airport approach course, failed to hear the local one controller's rundown on the departing Aero Commander, now climbing, almost abreast of the Pan Am 747, into the lower depths of the overcast.

Aboard the Aero Commander, now well into the clouds, a suddenly rough-running engine causes the pilot to fail to turn on his transponder. His position is displayed on the radar, but much less obviously than if his transponder had been turned on; there is no accompanying data block displaying his number, altitude, and groundspeed.

In the tower, the local one controller, anxious to depart Western 983, does not note that the departure controller failed to acknowledge his rundown on the Aero Commander.

As Western 983 begins his takeoff roll on 25 Right, Aero Commander 8637 Tango and Clipper five both level out within the overcast at 2,000.

As the Pan Am 747's data block appears on his radar, the departure controller issues his first instruction to the Pan Am pilot.

"Clipper five, Los Angeles departure, radar contact; maintain two thousand; turn left, heading one six zero."

"Maintain two; left turn to one six zero, Clipper five." acknowledges the Pan Am pilot, banking to the left. Unknowingly, he turns toward a collision course with Aero Commander 37 Tango, which is still level at 2,000 feet and maintaining its original runway heading of 250 degrees within the dense cloud.

At the departure one controller's position in the TRACON, Bill White, a controller detailed to training duties, stops to observe the trainee's progress. Not involved in the attempt to determine the position of the Beechcraft, he sees something on the radarscope no one else has noticed: the non-transponder target of Aero Commander 37 Tango several miles west of the airport on a 250 degree heading. To the right of this unidentified target, another target, identified by its data block as Clipper five, rapidly closes the distance between itself and the unknown plane.

"Who's that?" White quickly asks the departure trainee and his instructor, pointing his finger at the target representing 37 Tango and tapping the glass of the scope with his fingertip so there will be no misunderstanding.

"Who?" "Where?"

"HERE!" White says, anxiously tapping the creeping target's image on the scope as if somehow to crack the glass, reach through, and pluck the unidentified plane from the course of Clipper five.

"Turn Clipper now—'IMMEDIATE'—or you're gonna have a deal!" urges White, unable to contact the plane because he's not wearing a headset.

"*Clipper five, right turn IMMEDIATELY,*" orders the trainee, new to LAX, but still the best of the best at the busy facility he'd transferred from.

"Here's the other plane, Aero Commander 8637 Tango," the instructor quickly tells White while holding up the plane's flight clearance strip for White to read.

The only words White takes time to say are, "Turn him!"

This time the instructor is first to respond, "*Commander thirty-seven Tango, left turn IMMEDIATELY.*"

For the moment, there's no way of knowing whether either plane heard the controllers' instructions, or whether the imminent mid-air collision has already taken place. When a quick-thinking pilot receives an instruction containing the word "IMMEDIATE," he complies first and acknowledges later. His life depends on it. With agonizing slowness the bright line on the scope representing the sweep of the radar antenna moves clockwise toward its next contact with the targets of Clipper five and Aero Commander 37 Tango. As the antenna sweeps the previous positions of the two airplanes, their computer-updated targets spring forward—and touch. A split second later, the Boeing 747 pilot's voice fills the departure controllers' earphones:

"Clipper five, immediate right to two six zero, level two." The Pan Am pilot had done exactly the right thing at exactly the right moment; he'd immediately turned right, adding 90 degrees to the 170-degree heading he'd been "passing through" on his way toward the 160-degree heading he'd been given earlier.

The response of the Aero Commander pilot came next, "Three

seven Tango turning to one four zero, maintain two." He too had responded immediately and, in his acknowledgment, advised the controllers of his new heading and the fact that he was maintaining 2,000 feet. Both pilots knew that radar failure was an ever-present possibility and wanted the controller to know exactly what they were doing. Like many pilots, the Aero Commander pilot had pre-tuned his second radio before takeoff to the frequency he was next likely to need; in this case, departure control 124.3. He therefore heard the controller's call, even though the rough-running engine had kept him from the usual procedure of contacting departure after lift-off.

The two targets, too close for the radar to differentiate, parted after coming within a few feet of each other. Inside the heavy cloud, neither plane saw the other.

The thorough FAA investigation, begun almost immediately after the incident (the controllers involved were relieved within minutes), determined that primary responsibility for the near-collision rested with the local one controller in the tower who failed to obtain an acknowledgment, from departure, of his run-down on the Aero Commander. The FAA further determined that there were two contributing factors: the Beechcraft, which was believed to be on the LAX final approach course, distracted the departure controllers; and the Aero Commander pilot, preoccupied with the plane's rough-running engine, failed to turn on his transponder or to contact departure after lift-off.

Not included in the report was the knowledge all pilots and controllers have that, wherever there is the human element, there will—inevitably—be human errors. That possibility, and the intimate reaffirmation of his own potential for human error, each of the controllers involved would carry home, and back to work again, and perhaps into his dreams for the remainder of his career.

In the course of investigation, it was found that the Beechcraft, although 60 degrees from LAX, was so distant from the airport that it was well outside the TCA and far, far below the airport's final approach course when its pilot initially contacted departure control.

14 Los Angeles TRACON

The TRACON [Terminal Radar Approach Control] here is unusual. In most places where you have both easy and difficult jobs, the difficult jobs are usually the last ones filled when a shift changes. Here, the most demanding jobs are the first ones the guys go for coming on shift because they like to get in there and do their thing. After you've been on the position an hour, somebody's going to come up and say, 'Hey, you've had your hour!'

THE DEPARTURE controller who narrowly avoided the "deal" between Clipper five and Aero Commander 37 Tango was working one of four radar positions at LAX TRACON.

Arrival one handles arrivals from the east and southeast. Arrival one's main reporting fix for inbounds is noted on charts as "Downey" (after a nearby suburb); so, among controllers, arrival one is simply called "Downey."

Arrival two handles arrivals from the north and west. Named after its main reporting fix, arrival two is called "Stadium."

Departure one handles all traffic departing LAX south and

southeast, plus westbound jet departures.

Departure two is responsible for all LAX north and northeast, plus slow (prop) westbound departures.

Although there are plenty of potential nicknames for the departure positions they're merely referred to as "south departures" and "north departures." Downey and Stadium are the glamour positions.

There's one other radar position in the TRACON. It's manned only when parallel instrument approaches are being flown to any combination of LAX's four runways. Two controllers work the position. They use radar to monitor aircraft descending along the instrument-landing-system so that any plane which strays the slightest bit from any runway's approach-course-centerline can be immediately steered back on course, since 25 Left and 24 Right are less than a mile apart.

All of this, the arrival and departure and parallel approach positions, plus the watch supervisor's desk, and space for the computers and other equipment—and the twenty-four-hour-a-day, seven-day-a-week technical and maintenance staff assigned to keep the equipment working—are all housed in a building within a building. The single-story TRACON is seventy-five by fifty feet and is housed in a steel-braced, aluminum-walled, pre-fab structure wholly contained within an FAA hangar on the south side of Los Angeles International. The only time radar controllers at the TRACON get to see an airplane is on their day off or driving to or from work. The TRACON isn't staffed to provide time away for lunch, or for chalk-talks with trainees.

To the left, facing the room and radar positions like a long, narrow, off-center teacher's desk, is the watch supervisor's office without walls. Officially an assistant facility chief, he's hardly ever called anything but, "the A.C." Lighted by a single-bulb, gooseneck lamp, the A.C.'s desk is banked with enough buttons to please any Star Trek fan. There are five telephones in assorted colors, as though someone couldn't make up his mind which color to select and decided to take one of each. But it's all necessary for quick and simultaneous communication with scores of people and agencies in the event of emergency.

It takes your eyes a few moments to adjust to the near-darkness of the room beyond the circle of light cast by the lamp on the A.C.'s desk. At first, the only light in the forty- by twenty-foot room seems to come from four eighteen-inch radarscopes. There are two, barely six feet from each other, banked along each of the room's long walls to your left and right. Standing just inside the door by the A.C.'s desk, you can see little except the luminous, lime-green lines sweeping a complete, clockwise circle on the face of each radarscope every twelve seconds. If you're especially observant you soon note that, when the bright lines sweeping the scopes on your left are swinging past their tops, the lines circling on the two scopes to your right are closer to the four o'clock position. You guess there must be two radars, one feeding each pair of scopes. You're right.

As your eyes accommodate to the low-level light, dark shapes before the radarscopes resolve themselves into controllers, seated before and hunched up close to their radar displays in concentration which appears to, but which must not, exclude everything else taking place in the room. Stadium is close along the left wall, just beyond the A.C.'s desk. Downey is on Stadium's right. South and north departures are banked along the wall to your right; south departures back-to-back with Downey and north departures back-to-back with Stadium—although there's a space of about fifteen feet between the backs of controllers seated before the radars.

If Jules Verne had written *Twenty Thousand Leagues Under the Sea* today instead of during the 1870s, the TRACON could serve as the movie set for Captain Nemo's modern-day submarine.

Two controllers man each radar position: a radar controller who works the airplanes, and a flight-data controller who communicates with the computer via a typewriter-like keyboard, and who keeps track of each plane's flight strip detailing its assigned route, altitude, and transponder code. He also receives and makes hand-offs between the TRACON and other facilities. Every time a tower controller hands off a departing plane to departure control he talks to a departure flight-data controller. And, every time departure hands off an airplane to the en route center or any other facility, the flight-data man coordinates the hand-off. There's another controller working with each arrival and departure team—a coordinator stationed between the team's two radar controllers. Not directly involved in working airplanes, he's in a position to catch something a radar controller might miss—and he can assist a controller who's momentarily swamped. All these jobs: radar controller, flight-data controller, and coordinator are interchangeable and during his shift every controller will be called on to work more than one position.

Downey and Stadium are the pressure points and no one can maintain the high level of alertness and concentration required to work either for more than an hour—sixty minutes and you're off the position.

There's yet another controller assigned to each team: the team supervisor. Senior to the others by one pay grade, he doesn't rotate or normally work traffic. He's the team's boss and chief tactician when his team is swamped. And right now Downey and Stadium are swamped. It's the tail of the early evening arrival rush and there's a long line of inbounds descending out of the east toward LAX—seven minimum-spaced airliners inside the radar's twenty-five-mile-range mark, with others appearing at the edge of the Downey controller's radarscope like ducks in a shooting gallery, popping up one by one on a seemingly endless chain. Stadium is little better, north and west arrivals strung out eastbound north of LAX being "U-turned" inbound by the Stadium controller in a constant sequence of landings on whichever of the airport's four runways can take them.

To top it off, the man working Downey radar is a trainee—you don't learn to work heavy traffic by handling the position at five o'clock on Sunday morning.

"American three eighty-three," directs the trainee, *"maintain one eight zero knots to Lima;* [contact the] *tower there one one eight point nine. Keep six* [miles] *in trail* [of] *the seven zero seven ahead."*

The American flight is, so far, only tentatively assigned to one of the 25 runways, so the Downey controller has headed him toward Lima. The local one controller in the tower will assign American 383's landing runway.

"I think one six zero [knots] would be a better call," Joe Fowler, the team supervisor, advises.

"American three eighty-three," says the trainee, giving no hint that the instruction is anything more than routine, *"reduce speed further now to one six zero; maintain that until Lima."*

"American two eleven, one seven zero knots, cleared for the ILS [instrument landing system] *approach* [runway] *two four Left."*

"American two eleven, cleared for the approach two four Left."

"Make sure he's got the traffic," suggests Fowler.

"American two eleven, traffic is company [your airline] *DC-ten inbound for two four; do you see him?"*

"American two eleven, rog."

"American two eleven, do you see the traffic, sir?"

"That's affirm, American two eleven."

"O.K. two eleven, he's inbound for two four, are you light enough for two five Left?"

"Affirm, American two eleven."

"O.K., American two eleven, your runway's now two five Left, maintain one seven zero to Lima and visual separation on your company DC-ten ahead."

"American two eleven, to two five Left, visual on the company."

"American two eleven, reduce speed now to one six zero, maintain that to Lima."

"One six zero to Lima for American two eleven."

"You probably didn't need to do that," comments Fowler, "no sense sweating him if you don't have to.

"What about that Convair, 4080 Bravo?" asks Fowler, knowing the trainee's runway assignment for the forty-four-passenger corporate turboprop should be obvious.

"Two five Right to keep the Left open for wide-bodies."

"O.K."

"Convair forty-eighty Bravo, [maintain] *one six zero knots;*

cleared for the ILS two five Right."

"Cleared for the ILS, two five Right, eighty Bravo."

"Now what are you going to do with United four eighty-seven you got from Stadium?"

"Also two five Right for the same reason."

"Good, because you got American forty-one heavy you gotta put on two five Left."

"United four eighty-seven, maintain one six zero to Lima; cleared for the ILS two five Right."

"Maintain one six zero and cleared for the Right, United four eighty-seven."

"American forty-one heavy," the trainee asks just as Joe Fowler was about to prompt him, *"can you get below the United O.K.? He's on final for two five Right."*

"That's affirm, American forty-one."

"O.K., American forty-one, maintain one seven zero to Lima; tower there one one eight point nine."

"American forty-one, one seven zero to Lima."

"God damn! Look at the fuckin' turbo-prop Convair," somebody says, "he must have died over Lima, he's doin' one hundred knots—United four eighty-seven's eating him, you're gonna have a deal."

"Get four eighty-seven outta there," Fowler orders his trainee, "send him around!"

"I can't—he's changed [his radio] over to the tower!"

Immediately reaching forward between the radar controller and his data man, Joe Fowler presses the button which will connect him with the local one controller in the tower:

"Pull United Four eighty-seven outta there, immediate go-around, maintain altitude!"

"United four eighty-seven" orders the local one tower controller, not stopping even to wonder about the reason for the message he'd received, *"immediate go-around; maintain altitude; maintain runway heading; stay with me."*

"United four eighty-seven go-around," replies the DC-8 pilot.

Maintaining its 250-degree heading, the United DC-8 passes

directly over the airport less than 2,000 feet above the runways. The pilot retracted his plane's drag-producing landing gear as soon as he'd halted his rate of descent and now, as his plane heads out over the Pacific, he gradually changes the plane's flaps from landing to climb configuration.

"United four eighty-seven's going around," advises the local one controller.

"Yeah," answers Fowler, "we got him on the scope. Give him to departures."

"*O.K., United four eighty-seven, contact departure now one two four point three.*"

As the United pilot changes his radio from the tower to departure control frequency, Joe Fowler turns toward the A.C.'s desk, fifteen feet to his left:

"Hey, Jim," he calls, "you're gonna get a call from a mighty upset United pilot in a little while."

"Yeah?" the A.C. asks, walking over to the arrival control area, "What happened?"

What happened, what might have caused a mid-air collision, was silent, subtle, and at the time, invisible.

Shortly before the Convair began its final descent, part of the transparent layer-cake of air close to the surface, somewhere between 400 and 1,500 feet above the ground, began to move. While instruments on the ground registered no change at all, the eastward-flowing mass of air between 400 and 1,500 feet quickly and invisibly attained a speed of perhaps 40 knots. If it had continued, the adjoining air above and below would have begun to move too, caught up in the current—and there would have been some warning. If there had been tall smokestacks near the airport someone in the tower might have noticed smoke lazily drifting upward, then suddenly caught and bent horizontal as it penetrated the rapidly moving air mass. As it was, the mini-wind shear soon became visible on the radar as the groundspeed, indicated by the data blocks of plane descending into the shear, began to show a 40-knot decrease.

The A.C. was standing behind the Downey radar controller

along with the team supervisor and the coordinator from departure.

"Now look at American 383," said Joe Fowler, as much to the other controllers gathered at the position as to his trainee, "he's showing 140 knots on the glideslope inside Lima, you can go by that.

"Now you watch Continental 31 behind him showing 180 knots at 2,800. He'll come back—there he goes passing through 2,000: 170 . . . 160 . . . 150 . . . 140 . . . 140—that's it; you got a 40-knot wind shear out there.

"What that means is that we have to increase our separation now to seven, maybe eight, miles instead of three to five because we know when they pass through 2,000 they'll be dyin' and whoever's behind will be closing up on them."

With a fully-qualified controller taking the trainee's place at the radar, Fowler continues:

"What you've got to do, is not so much watch the groundspeed as just watch the target and the spacing. Remember, what you're doing all this for is to provide separation; that's what you watch: separation.

"A wind shear like that is just one more thing you've got to live with, kid."

"Hey, Fowler," asks the departure coordinator, chiding the arrival team supervisor for his lecture, "you been smoking grass?"

"Yeah!"

"Hey Strother," calls someone from the A.C.'s desk, "there's a United captain on the phone wants to talk to the watch supervisor!"

15   Downey

As a controller, your voice has got to be like a surgeon's hands. That surgeon doing an operation might be scared as hell; he might be so nervous he's screaming at everybody; or he might even be drinking too much, but, when he's in that operating room, his hand has got to be rocksteady. When you're working traffic you've got to sound cool; and you've got to sound sure and authoritative. When you screw up, or somebody else screws up, and you've got to do something fast or you're going to have a mid-air, your 'Continental 233, left turn to 190,' has got to sound like the most routine communication in all the world.

DOWNEY AND Stadium are the pressure points. Departure one and two handle just as much traffic—since every plane landing at LAX eventually takes off—but arrival control (called *approach* by pilots and controllers) brings planes together for landing on closely-spaced runways, while departure disperses them to widely separated destinations. Downey and Stadium, and even departure one and departure two, are two-man positions, but Downey is more of a two-man position than any of

the others. Since the FAA doesn't staff for positions vacated during lunch breaks or during chalk-talks, Stadium must often be
worked by one controller. Downey never is; it's too hard to handle. If you wash out in the TRACON, you wash out on Downey.
The radar controller on the position "works" the traffic; talking
to pilots—assigning headings and altitudes and airspeeds. In controller jargon, he "makes the calls." The primary job of the second
controller working the position is to talk to the FAA computer
and to other facilities "handing off" airplanes to Downey.

Until a few years ago, radarscopes were mounted horizontally
so that plastic "shrimp boats," bearing the same information as
data blocks, could be pushed around on the scope helping controllers to identify the aircraft. And hand-offs were made by telephone. Today, data blocks displayed on the radarscope showing
the flight number, altitude, and ground speed of each airplane are
a function of the computer. Hand-offs are also made and accepted
through the computer. The FAA's computer on the ground is in
constant contact with an electronic transponder (transmitter-
responder) in each airplane.

The transponder has the ability to transmit (squawk) any one
of 4,096 codes, and, before takeoff, each plane departing or arriving at LAX is assigned a specific code to squawk. With each plane
squawking a different transponder code, the FAA radar-computer
link can tell one plane from another and show the appropriate data
blocks next to each plane's target on the scope. Every time the
radar controller accepts a hand-off, he'll tell the pilot to "ident."
The pilot then presses a button on his transponder which causes
his data block to blink for twenty seconds on the controller's
scope. As soon as he sees the data block begin to blink, the
controller can safely tell the pilot, "radar contact." If the data
block doesn't blink, the controller knows the transponder isn't
functioning properly, or that he's not in communication with the
pilot. In any case, he's forewarned that he has to devote extra
attention to that plane until he's in contact with the pilot. The
transponder has another feature. If a pilot has an in-flight emergency, the transponder can be set to blink his data block continu-

ously to catch the controller's attention. At the same time, the word "EMER" appears as part of the plane's data block.

Apart from following regulations, there's no standard way of working the position—and the shades of difference are subtle. A strong hand-off man can set things up so well that the radar controller is sometimes left with relatively little to do. By working closely with the en route center; that is, handing off the long line of arrivals closely in trail, the hand-off man brings almost every plane onto the radar controller's scope perfectly spaced from the one ahead of it. And if an extra space has to be made in the long line of east arrivals to accommodate an airplane approaching from the south, or one that must be handed off by Stadium to Downey, the hand-off man can ask the en route center to slow down the speed of inbound aircraft and the rate of hand-offs. In this way, the "hole" which the radar controller needs appears, as if by magic, in the line of arrivals at the edge of his radarscope.

On the other hand, there are very sharp controllers who'll tell you they could work Downey without any hand-off man at all. You have to believe them, Stadium has to be worked that way far too often.

It's late Friday afternoon, the height of the arrival rush, and the team supervisor, Bill Boyle, has two of the team's best controllers working Downey. Sam Rose, thirty-two and of slight build with almost wild, red hair and beard, is radar controller. Dave Gourley is hand-off man, a bearded Burl Ives with voice to match, or perhaps an oversized Ernest Hemingway. Gourley, at forty-one, is the oldest controller in the TRACON; however, Boyle, a few years younger than Gourley, has been there longer.

For the past thirty minutes traffic has been coming faster than the airport can accept it and Gourley has asked the en route center to slow both the speed of inbound airplanes and the rate of hand-offs.

Soon the en route center's three lines of inbounds will be backed eastward across the sky all the way to Las Vegas and perhaps beyond. But there is little that Rose and Gourley can do except ask for the slowdown when airlines insist on scheduling more arrivals during a given hour than the airport can accept. Listening to the running dialogue between the two men, you have no doubt about their mutual respect and smooth working relationship. To do their best together each has to know what the other is thinking and feeling.

"Dave, I want to see if we can pull TWA two twenty-nine outta that line for two five and put him over on two four because he's getting bounced around a bit by that wide-body, American three eighty-three up ahead of him."

"Stadium; Downey," Gourley contacts the Stadium hand-off controller on his headset (intercom link), "can you take TWA two twenty-nine for two four?"

"Yup," answers the Stadium hand-off man, glancing at his radarscope—which shows the same picture that Downey's shows.

"TWA two twenty-nine," directs Rose, *"change your runway now to two four; contact Los Angeles approach one two eight point five."*

"TWA two twenty-nine, change to two four; approach one two eight point five."

"O.K., Dave, getting rid of the TWA gives us a hole we can put Japan thirty-four into. He's going to the cargo terminals on the south side."

Gourley talks to Stadium and takes Japan 34, a stretch DC-8, for 25 Left. Nobody keeps score, but you like to keep things even; now it's an even trade—Japan 34 for TWA 229.

"Japan thirty-four," says the Stadium radar controller to the DC-8 which he soon would have had to turn inbound for 24, *"contact Los Angeles approach now one two four point nine."*

"Los Angeles approach, Japan thirty-four," the Japan Airlines pilot responds after changing his radio from Stadium's frequency to Downey's.

"Japan thirty-four, Los Angeles, right turn now to intercept the runway two five localizer."

"Japan thirty-four."

There are almost simultaneous landings on all four runways now. Standing in the middle of the airport looking east, you could count the landing lights of twenty airliners—four strings of five each—in sight for landing on 24 Left and 24 Right, and 25 Left and 25 Right. Taking the size of the airplanes into account, there's little more distance between runway pairs than between the landing decks of aircraft carriers tied side by side. Too often airliners will touch down almost at the same time, jet fighter style, side by side on nearby runways. Any problem with one—a blown tire or brake that grabs—could instantly involve both.

Rose and Gourley are prisoners of the system now, caught in a pressure cooker of speeding airliners and thousands of lives coming together in less space and time than the airport or its air traffic controllers were ever meant to handle. It's the only ball game in the world where you always have to bat a thousand.

"American three eighty-three," says Sam Rose to a 707 which is too quickly closing the distance between itself and a TWA flight ahead, *"do not pass that DC-ten. You can maintain visual separation, but do not pass him, please. He's reduced to one eight zero now, landing two five Left. Your runway's two five Right."*

"American three eighty-three, roger, we won't pass him."

"Sam," suggests Dave Gourley, "how 'bout we see if we can move American forty-one over to two four to save ourselves two miles on final?"

"Yeah, that's good."

Gourley contacts Stadium and makes the transfer. A few seconds later Rose contacts American 41 with the runway change.

"American forty-one, Los Angeles approach, can you change over to two four please?"

"American forty-one, roger."

"O.K., American forty-one, intercept the runway two four localizer now and contact approach one two eight point five."

"American forty-one, so long."

"Los Angeles approach, United seventy-seven with you, ten thousand," calls an airliner which the en route center has just handed off to Downey. As United 77 appeared at the edge of Downey's radarscope, its data block was blinking—the en route center's way of saying, via computer, "We're handing you United seventy-seven."

One of Gourley's tools as hand-off man is called a "trackball"; often it's quicker to use than the typewriter computer terminal in front of him. The hand-off man's trackball is black, and about the size of a billiard ball. Only the top quarter protrudes above the horizontal portion of Gourley's hand-off position beside the radar controller. By rolling the trackball in its socket, he can move a brightly-glowing, lime-green "U" anyplace on the Downey radar-scope. Rolling the trackball now, slewing the "U" to the radar target representing United 77, Gourley briefly presses the "enter" key on his console, and United 77's data block ceases to blink. Continuously glowing now on the radarscopes at both Downey and the en route center, it confirms to both controllers that the hand-off has been accepted by Downey.

There are separate instrument landing systems at LAX for each set of runways. Click-stopping his navigational radio's frequency selector to 109.9, the pilot tunes to the runway 25 ILS. He'll follow that beam, which is halfway between 25 Left and 25 Right, until he's assigned one runway or the other for landing. Under low visibility conditions, he'd follow it to within a few hundred feet of the ground and then have to slew left or right to his assigned runway. A four-ILS arrangement, one for each LAX runway, would be safer, but that's in the future.

"Los Angeles approach, Delta eleven twenty-five with you outta ten thousand."

Again, as Gourley slews his computer-connected trackball to accept the hand-off, Sam Rose answers the pilot:

"Delta eleven twenty-five, Los Angeles approach, radar contact; maintain one eight zero; intercept the localizer runway two five."

"Delta eleven twenty-five slowing to one eight zero; intercept the localizer for two five."

"United seventy-seven, descend to seven thousand."

"United seventy-seven, outta ten for seven."

"Sam, Stadium wants to know if you can take PSA seven

twenty-four; I told 'em you'd be more than happy."

"I'll build a hole for the PSA between United seventy-seven and the Delta."

Pressing the button on his console which connects his headset with the en route center controller who is working hand-offs to Downey, Gourley asks, "How 'bout you guys slowing down the next couple of airplanes to one seven zero?"

"We'll do it!" says the center's hand-off controller.

While Dave Gourley was talking to the center, Rose was already beginning to build his hole for PSA 724.

"Delta eleven twenty-five, reduce speed now to one seven zero. Expect descent to seven thousand in twenty miles."

"Delta eleven twenty-five slowing to one seven zero."

What Sam Rose told the Delta pilot in the between-the-lines language of pilots and controllers was, "You better get it slowed down pretty damn quick, because in a few minutes I'm going to issue your descent and we both know it's hell to slow it down and descend at the same time."

At the next sweep of the radar antenna, Delta 1125's data block shows he's slowed to 175 knots. Rose knows that, at the following antenna sweep, 1125 will be slowed to 170 and he can descend the airliner to 7,000. "That Delta pilot's O.K.," he thinks, "thank God for small favors."

"United seventy-seven," says Rose now turning his attention to the plane ahead of Delta 1125, *"your runway's two five Right; begin your final descent now; maintain one eight zero to Lima; tower there one one eight point nine."*

"United seventy-seven, outta seven, maintain one eight zero to Lima."

With United 77 maintaining his 180-knot groundspeed and Delta 1125 slowed to 170 knots, the space between the two airplanes slowly begins to open, creating the ten-mile "hole" Rose will need to slip PSA 724 between United and Delta. Looking at Stadium's traffic, Rose sees that PSA 724 is the second plane Stadium will have to turn toward the airport. The hole he needs for the PSA is growing, but not fast enough. But he can't leave

Delta 1125 at 10,000 feet all day either.

"Delta eleven twenty-five, descend to seven thousand; maintain one seven zero; intercept the localizer runway two five."

"Delta eleven twenty-five goin' to seven, intercept the runway two five ILS.'

At the edge of the scope the target and blinking data block for American 211 appear, its ground speed a glowing 170. No problem there at least.

"Los Angeles approach, American two eleven, ten thousand."

"American two eleven, Los Angeles, radar contact maintain one seven zero; expect descent in twenty miles."

"American two eleven."

Rose realizes that within two minutes at the most Stadium will have to turn PSA 724 and that he'd better have a place to put him. His hole for 724 is bigger now, but still not big enough. He'll have to take advantage of the Delta pilot, who seems like he knows what he's doing, anyway:

"Delta eleven twenty-five, if feasible, reduce speed now to one six zero; maintain that to Lima."

"Delta eleven twenty-five, slowing to one six zero."

"That should do it," Rose says to himself, then adding, "It better."

If the traffic weren't so heavy, or if he wasn't hemmed in on every side by airspace belonging to other people—to nearby airports and their approach controllers with *their* problems, he could turn Delta 1125 a few degrees off the final approach course and then turn him back on again. Vectoring is a standard technique, but here there's very little airspace he can use; so speed control is just about his only tool. He has to start American 211 down:

"American two eleven, descend and maintain seven thousand; if feasible, maintain one seven zero knots." It won't be easy, but the American pilot can do it.

"One seven zero to seven thousand, American two eleven."

"Thanks, two eleven," offers Rose.

"Click—click," the 211's pilot quickly presses his microphone's transmit button twice in succession. When the frequency is too congested for unessential words, this signal is pilot-to-controller, not-quite-silent-language for "You're welcome,"

"PSA seven twenty-four," says Stadium to the 727 which he's handing off to Downey, *"contact Los Angeles approach now one two four point nine."*

"Seven twenty-four," the PSA pilot responds, changing to Downey's radio frequency.

"Los Angeles approach, PSA seven twenty-four."

"PSA seven twenty-four, Los Angeles, turn right to intercept the runway two five localizer; cleared for the ILS two five approach; maintain one six zero to Lima; tower one one eight point nine there."

"PSA seven twenty-four, one six zero to Lima."

That was a lot to give the PSA pilot at once, but PSA flies in and out of LAX a hundred times a day and the pilot of 724 has probably landed here a thousand times. You can count on PSA.

Noting the tight situation with the not quite big enough hole for PSA 724 between United 77 and Delta 1125, Dave Gourley called the tower and got a guaranteed runway 25 Left assignment for the Delta. Now it would be O.K.—not great, but O.K.—if the Delta should happen to close up a bit behind the PSA which will be landing on 25 Right.

United 77's for 25 Left; then PSA for 25 Right; then Delta 1125 on 25 Left. It will work and the tower should be able to get one departure off each runway between landings.

"God damn," Rose exclaims, "the fuckin' radar's gone out again!"

In five steps the arrival team supervisor is at the A.C.'s desk: "Jim, our radar's out."

"O.K., I'll call maintenance next door."

In two or three minutes, maintenance technicians will be swarming over the radar equipment located in an adjoining room, which is larger than the air traffic side of the TRACON and houses the radar terminals and computers that produce the aircraft targets and data blocks used by controllers. But a lot can happen in minutes; you can have a deal, a couple of deals, in minutes.

Fortunately, it hasn't been a total failure. The radar picture's still there, but, instead of enhanced targets converted by the computer into symbols representing various categories of airplanes, there is only a misty radarscope with ghostly images representing the crisp targets which until seconds ago precisely pinpointed airplanes. The data blocks are gone along with their altitude and groundspeed data. Dave Gourley's trackball doesn't work, and there are no flashing data blocks to indicate a plane is being handed off to Downey. Suddenly, working as hand-off man has become more than a full-time job.

Sam Rose's job was already more than full-time, and now he's got to guess each plane's airspeed—and ask pilots over and over again to tell him their altitude. Merging targets, which moments ago were of no consequence because their data blocks showed thousands of feet altitude separation, now become a compelling concern: every plane he's working must now be warned of possibly conflicting traffic:

"American two twenty-one, say altitude now passing."

"Delta eleven twenty-five, possible traffic, twelve o'clock, four miles; altitude unknown."

"PSA seven twenty-four, traffic for runway two four, nine o'-clock, two miles; altitude unknown."

"United seventy-seven, say altitude."

"Delta eleven twenty-five, say your airspeed now."

"PSA seven twenty-four, say your airspeed."

The data blocks come back; fade; then come back and stay on. Nobody knows for how long.

"Even if the damned thing worked 97 percent of the time," remarks the arrival coordinator, "it would still be like having to fight 100 duels a day aware that three of your bullets were duds, but never knowing which ones."

"Coming to work in this place," says the Stadium radar controller, "is like walking down a dark alley on the wrong side of town at midnight. You never know if you'll make it."

At 6:30, just the time PSA 724 was scheduled to touch down after its non-stop flight from San Francisco, a giant, long-range, three-engine British Airways DC-10, heavy with fuel and passengers for its non-stop flight to London, departed runway 24 Left.

As Sam Rose orchestrated his traffic along the 25 approach course to make a hole for PSA 724, British Airways flight 598 was handed off by the tower to departure control.

A few minutes later, as Rose and Gourley and every other controller in the TRACON were struggling with the day's third —or was it fourth—partial radar failure, the British Airways pilot found he had a problem, a problem announced by the fire warning alarm for one of his three engines.

The first thing that caught every controller's eyes when the radar came back on was the blinking data block for British Airways 598. With it was the word "EMER." Every radar controller in range of 598's transponder knew the flight was in trouble. The pilot of 598 hadn't spoken to Sam Rose—the plane was still on departure control frequency; so it was the departure controller who received first word from the pilot. Nobody had to tell Gourley and Rose that they'd soon be handling the flight. With an in-flight emergency he wasn't going to London. He'd be back on the ground as soon as he could.

It was Jim Strother, the assistant chief, who informed the arrival team, referring to the flight by its air traffic control "handle" rather than by its company name:

"Speedbird five ninety-eight's coming back. He's got a fire warning light and he's shut number three down."

The DC-10 could fly well enough on two of its three engines, but it was heavy, too heavy for a go-around if that became necessary, and too heavy, also, to safely stop on the runway with only two of its engines' thrust reversers available to help the plane brake after touchdown. So Speedbird 598 would circle for a time, dumping a hundred thousand pounds or so of excess fuel, before returning to LAX. In-flight emergencies often come in threes, so the DC-10 might call for immediate landing clearance at any moment. In the meantime, it remained a distracting time bomb ticking away in a corner of each controller's mind.

In the tower across the airport from the TRACON, the watch supervisor began alerting LAX firefighters, airport security, the city fire department (to provide ambulances), city police (to clear traffic), the Coast Guard, and every other agency which could help save lives in the event the plane was unable to reach the airport, or went crashing off the far end of its landing runway, or overshot the runway and, unable to climb, crashed into the sea just west of the field.

The planes which Rose and Gourley had been working landed, only to be followed by others which continued to appear, flashing for attention, at the edge of the Downey radar. The only way to handle the traffic was as if the situation were normal; yet very soon Downey would receive a call from Speedbird 598 and the stricken plane would take precedence over everything.

And the radar, everyone knew, might go out again at any time.

16   Sam Rose

The FAA management doesn't care and doesn't do a damn thing to alleviate what's tearing up controllers. You can write memos about problems, but nobody really gives a shit—nobody except the poor bastard who has to work the traffic. But management never listens to him because he's just a dumb controller who doesn't have the "big picture" and his viewpoint doesn't count. If the flying public knew about the deficiencies in the system and the conditions we work under, they'd be staying home and writing their Congressmen.

AT THIRTY-TWO, Sam Rose has devoted most of his working life to air traffic control: four years in the Marine Corps, including time in Viet Nam, and seven years, since 1971, in the FAA as a controller in Florida and California.

"I got into air traffic control," he says, "because when I went into the Marines I had a choice of going to parachute rigger school in New Jersey or to air traffic control (ATC) school in Glencoe, Georgia. I didn't know anything then about air traffic control, but I knew Georgia was close to Florida; so I said air traffic control school was fine by me. You really can't compare being a controller in the Marines with being an FAA controller. The training was better in the Marines and you had the feeling somebody cared about your working conditions and about safety.

"But, even in the FAA, controlling airplanes *can* be fun. It's a kick in the butt to sit down there at the position when you're just busier than hell and everything goes right, when the radios are working and the radar's working and you take that bowl of popcorn and throw it up in the air and it comes down—strung! It's neat and it makes you feel good—a sense of accomplishment— your speed control, your spacing, your phraseology impeccable. It works out perfectly and you feel good about it. But just as often you come in and you're two people short and the radios don't work and the radar keeps going out. The system is very unreliable and not what the FAA builds it up to be.

"The computer keyboard has to be handled just right and if you even look at it sideways you have to go back and cancel and re-type the keyboard entry; and you're always using the damn thing—every time there's a change in any plane's flight plan or a million and one other things. So you go back and change the keyboard entry. Now your attention is diverted from the control of airplanes to working the keyboard and trying to get the computer to show you a flight number and altitude and groundspeed which you have to remember anyway in case the damn thing breaks down and the data blocks go off. Then, when it does go off, the A.C. has to pull the new men off the busy positions and put on the old hands who've had experience with the older type radar that didn't have data blocks because the A.C. realizes that if anything happens there will be an investigation and somebody will say, 'You mean you had controllers available who were experienced with the non-computer system and you didn't use them and instead you used new controllers who were inexperienced with a non-computer system? Why, you're negligent!'

"There's more emphasis on political implications in the FAA than upon safety, and I can name several cases right here at LAX:

"Number one: after midnight, for 'noise-abatement,' we have

all takeoffs going out to the *west* and all landings to the *east;* so you have a plane taking off west, and sitting out there in the sky, right in front of him, is another plane, head-on, that's going to land to the east, on the same runway. I can't tell you how many near-misses we've had. Landing to the east at night also makes the pilots descend into a 'black hole' over the water that robs them of the visual cues they need for a good, stabilized descent. We also often get a fog drifting in over the west end of the runways at night and landing to the east forces pilots to land into that. We've already had one serious accident because of the nightime east landings and the controllers and the Air Line Pilots Association complain and complain about it but the FAA doesn't do anything. There's only one 'safest' way to operate the airport and that's not it.

"Number two: the FAA is under a lot of political pressure to put more minorities to work as controllers. That's fine; I'm for it and every controller I know is for it. The problem is that when a minority person isn't able to qualify on a position in the allotted number of hours' training, somebody comes along and says, 'Oh well, those hours weren't actually representative hours,' and they get more time and still more time. And when you get certified on a position it's not supposed to be on the basis of any single performance rating but on a truly representative series of performances. So what you have now is a case of people who don't have the talent or the ability, or whatever you want to call it, being given extra time, and then often being certified on the basis of a single, barely competent performance instead of sustained performance. Someone in management needs to say that everybody has to meet the same standards. Any departure from that ties up competent controllers in training people who don't have the ability, and, worse, it puts individuals in jobs where they're in a position to kill people. I know the subject is unpopular; I know it's unpleasant; and I know it sounds bigoted. But it's a fact. And journeyman controllers will confirm it and it's dangerous and it should be stopped. But, because of politics, it probably won't be.

"Trying to get anything done working through management

is an unbelievable hassle. Soon after I got to Los Angeles I noticed that our radios couldn't override the pilots'; that is, if an airline pilot was talking away on the frequency and we had to tell somebody, 'Immediate right turn!' to avoid a mid-air, we couldn't do it. We'd just have to wait until he was through because the plane's transmitter was more powerful than ours. We had 10 watts and the airliners have 25. So I went to management and said, 'Our having only 10 watts is really dangerous, let us go back to 50 watts.' And do you know what they said?—that they didn't know we had only 10 watts of power. I told the management I knew we only had 10 watts because I read the notice which came around that said we had only 10 watts. So then they did a little checking and, sure enough, we had only 10 watts of power. So then they said, 'Controller Rose, are you sure this is a valid problem?' I said, 'I'm telling you it's a valid problem,' but they wouldn't accept my word for it. So we did a study for three weeks, and they finally agreed that maybe I had something there. 'But there's nothing we can do about it,' they told me, 'because it's Washington policy and every air traffic facility is down to 10 watts; so you guys will have to live with it.' I told them they were wrong and called the regional office and made an appointment with somebody in engineering. I went up there and told him what management said and he told me, 'We can get you back 50 watts any time you want.' So we finally got 50 watts on 124.9 and 124.5, our primary approach control frequencies. But it was a hassle with our own management every inch of the way.

"Undoubtedly one of the worst morale factors among controllers is the feeling that, while a high degree of professionalism is demanded of us, the bureaucracy is only really interested in politics and expanding their scope of influence and control. When you have thousands of controllers coming to work every day pissed off at the FAA it can't help but affect safety.

"We're tossing so many numbers around all the time: 'PSA 724,' 'clear for the ILS approach runway 24,' 'wind 200,' [degrees] 'maintain flight level 200,' 'United 118,' 'contact the tower now 118.9'; yet, if you make one mis-call, you can jeopardize people's lives. You just can not say, 'TWA twenty-five, turn left to two seven zero, descend and maintain five thousand,' when you should have said, 'TWA twenty-five, turn left to two five zero and descend and maintain seven thousand.' The call isn't that obviously bad and the TWA pilot will do it—and, unless you're perfect, you will run two planes together before you know what's happened. And —man—you *know* you're not perfect. You try very hard to be a perfectionist; a good controller is a controller who does everything right. But every day you live with the potential consequences of the fact that you're *not* perfect. And if the radar goes out three times on a shift and you're short-staffed as we so often are, you go home frustrated and angry. "You can't get rid of that frustration because it's a permanent part of the job—that just happens to be the way it is.

"Normally when we've had bad days, which come to think of it is almost every day, a bunch of us from the TRACON stop by the Red Onion down in Huntington Beach and drink a lot and talk it over, argue about it and yell and scream and by the time ten o'clock rolls around we're so soused we can't be coherent anymore or make sense about what we were saying, so we just table it and drive home. Air traffic control would be a great job for a professional bachelor. Marriage is an added responsibility and you have to accommodate yourself to your wife's feelings and responsibilities. Maybe my wife, Joanne, has had a bad day too, and if I've had a bad day it isn't fair for me to come home and push my bad day on Joanne's already bad day; so I have to get it out of my system before I come home in order for Joanne and me to get along. Joanne and I live aboard our 45-foot ketch, and, if she 'errs' and leaves on a 12-volt light, I'll say, 'Why did you leave that on?' and she'll say, 'I forgot.' Well, to me that doesn't represent a 'valid excuse,' but that's a work attitude which isn't appropriate at home and which causes friction between us. The demand for perfectionism is not a desirable *personal* attitude, but in air traffic control it's a very desirable *professional* attitude.

"Perfection is expected of us always, but if anything happens where a controller's not negligent, not incompetent, but simply not absolutely perfect, his own management will jump on his back saying, 'This controller did not follow prescribed air traffic control procedures,' and he'll be penalized. Well, the air traffic control procedures in the FAA's book are set up *politically* to protect the FAA and management. It is absolutely and totally impossible for the Los Angeles TRACON or any other busy facility in the United States to operate within the procedures set down in that book. It is impossible to do it. Whenever the public reads about a so-called air traffic controller slowdown, the only slowdown is that the controllers are going 100 percent by the book. The rest of the time they are putting their careers on the line because regulations are violated every day, day in and day out, in order to handle the volume of airplanes that we have to handle. I think most controllers will admit their mistakes, but it pisses you off when, in spite of all the evidence, the pilots who are supposedly working with you won't admit theirs.

"Yesterday afternoon when I was working departure a United DC-10 came off 24 Left and he drifted way south of the 25 departure course and I said, 'United 108, did you get a heading from the tower after departure?', and he said 'No.' So I said, 'Well, did you encounter a lot of wind [from the north] after you departed?' And he said, 'No.' And I said, 'Well, the reason I'm asking is that you drifted a mile south of the 25 departure course and I just wondered how you got there.' So he said, 'We had this airplane all set up on the runway heading and we couldn't have drifted south!' I said, 'Well, all I'm trying to do is find out if there's some wind where you are because there are more airplanes going to take off behind you and if they're all going to drift south I want to be prepared for it.' And he came back with, 'Well, we had this airplane all set up and I don't think what you're saying is correct.'

"Of course, all of us could see on the radar exactly where he was; so, when we handed him off to the center, I said that I appreciated his cooperation in the spirit of safer aviation and to have a nice day in the friendly skies.

"Not long before the DC-10 situation, I had a problem with

an American jet that made me lose my temper—which I shouldn't have done. I had taken over the departure one radar position and there were a number of airplanes climbing out in trail, with this one American climbing slow and flying slow. The only way to solve it was pull the American out of the line; so I turned him to the right a few degrees and he says, 'How come we have to do this?' "So I answered that 'Due to the poor performance of your aircraft, traffic behind you is overtaking you, and I have to take you out of the departure line and put you on a parallel course to the south.' He got all hot and bothered and testy about it, and I lost my temper and fairly well jumped his poop. He complained; his airline complained; and so we had to go to the daily tape and there it was. I said it was a mistake on my part to lose my temper and a mistake on my part to say something that I shouldn't have said on the air.

"But the fact remains that the way I handled the traffic was right; the pilot was saying I was wrong. I told the management that if American Airlines didn't feel I handled the air traffic situation right, then American should write a letter showing how it could have been handled in a better way than I'd handled it— because American complained I'd handled it poorly. I handled my emotional maturity poorly, but the air traffic situation American was complaining about I did not handle poorly.

"If everything isn't done when and how it should be by both controllers and pilots, it isn't going to work. It's not just that one airliner that doesn't fit—now the next guy has to slow down; now the one behind him has to be turned out of line; now this one gets a runway change. Then it affects the center because they have to start slowing the traffic down. Soon it affects every other sector in the room because each controller is twice as busy trying to salvage as much as he can and make a new plan for his original plan that now isn't going to work. Now, everybody's busier than they should be and the whole damn thing snowballs and affects everybody.

"If the FAA would insist that safety is our most important

product instead of trying to handle everything on a political basis, that attitude would filter through the system and people would be motivated to produce a safe end result. Now, almost everybody's first priority is covering their ass politically if something happens."

17   Joanne Rose

I think, generally, that controllers have a difficult time relating to women in any manner other than as a stereo-type wife or sex partner kind of relationship. They seem to be trying to prove to themselves that they're real men.

"**A** GOOD CONTROLLER has to be a perfectionist—a man who doesn't make mistakes at work, who can't make mistakes—and he feels that responsibility very much. There *is* a lot of pressure and they *do* know they're not perfect; and it's frightening. When they've had a hard day they release their tension at a bar after work and later, when they come home, they have nothing to talk about. There are still a lot of tensions that overflow at home and that affects the relationship. I try to learn not to get upset about it, but I think that in so doing it kind of makes me not as sympathetic a person as before because when you shut yourself off from something you kind of turn off part of yourself and it becomes harder and harder to turn back on again.

"The rotating shift schedule that controllers work is probably responsible more than anything else for the very high divorce rate you see among controllers. When a man is working two days of days, two days of evenings, and then one midnight shift, it not only leaves him constantly exhausted with his whole body never really at peace with itself, but it also makes it extremely difficult for his wife or mate to have a career or serious interests of her own if she wants to have time with him. There are no careers that I know of where you can work the kinds of hours the FAA demands of controllers. I suppose it might be possible if a woman wanted to be a retail sales clerk in a big discount store, but not every woman wants to clerk in a store. Certainly there are no professional positions available, even if the FAA's work schedule weren't so physiologically detrimental and you wanted to work those hours.

"I know the FAA management probably thinks its schedule is fine; it certainly looks neat and well-ordered when you look at it taped to our refrigerator door, but it's damaging to *people,* and it's damaging to relationships, and neither one of those effects can be left entirely behind when a controller goes to work. They are stress points which, if anyone were to look closely enough, might be at the root of some of the 'controller error' which the government is listing as the cause, or partial cause, of fatal airline accidents.

"I think that for a controller's marriage to survive you have to have a relationship where the husband and wife each have their separate identities and interests, as well as their interests together, that the wife not be dependent upon her husband for her identity. Then, I think, the work schedule which separates them would not affect the marriage as much as it would in a relationship where the wife is just Mrs. John Smith. One reason so many controllers' wives resent the frequent separation is that they're always the ones at home waiting; they are the 'separatees,' always being left out of life. In our case I'm away just as much of the time with my schooling as Sam is away at work. Since we have that kind of situation, Sam can understand how it feels to be at home waiting for me, and I can understand Sam's side of it also—sometimes wanting to stop off on the way home. The fact that we do have separate identities has helped us. It will be different when I start work, and it is very different for the wife who has children and who is home all the time. She's always got to be there and can't get babysitters to match his crazy schedule and if she wants to get involved in something it's very hard to do. So he goes to work and comes home and she stays in the house and they just settle into their ways.

"The woman's frustration comes out in different ways. I know controllers whose wives are pushing them very hard to get ahead in the FAA hierarchy—just like mothers pushing children for straight "A"s or to be child movie stars. That's just another pressure on the husband that he doesn't need. Other wives take out their resentment by becoming frigid. For whatever reason, I think it's somewhat common for controllers to be, shall we say, 'unfaithful' to their wives. Controllers themselves are a very tight group and, if the husband is running around, he'll bring his 'runee-around-with' to controller parties and his wife will never know. But everyone else will.

"Because of the work hours, almost all your husband's friends tend to be controllers and when couples do get together the men talk about airplanes and the women talk to each other. Controllers even tend to close themselves off from other controllers at different facilities. The controllers at LAX tower and LAX TRACON don't even go to the same bars or see very much of each other. When Sam first took me to the TRACON to see how it was, the person who was giving me the tour asked me if I understood what was going on and I said, 'Well, sort of, I've seen an operation like this when Sam was working at Long Beach,' and the controller said, 'Oh, this is different. This is nothing at all like Long Beach!' Well, of course, it is different, but it's basically the same thing; the same element. But they were so aghast that I could think their operation was anything like Long Beach.

"I think there's a lot of resentment on the part of older controllers when a young controller gets checked out in a short time. The older controllers seem to be holding the younger ones back, not letting them check out. It's like, 'Well, nobody can check out here that easy,' because, after all, if a younger controller can check out in a short time, how super can the older controller really be?

"A lot of the younger men coming into the FAA the past few years seem to be more enlightened and have more varied interests than the old-timers. I think Sam is one of the first of the new breed."

18 We Just Lost Golden West 261!

I don't know to this day why I didn't see that other airplane on the radar. It didn't show at all, but when I lost radar contact with the airliner, a gut feeling told me I'd had a mid-air.

T HE COMMUTER airline flight which took the lives of ten passengers and two crew members was a short one. Golden West Airlines flight 261 departed Ontario International Airport about fifty miles east of Los Angeles at 3:56 P.M. Eleven minutes later, at 4:07 P.M., the lives of everyone aboard abruptly ended when the twin-engine airliner and a single-engine training plane met in midair over Whittier, California. Wreckage of the collision, which also took the lives of the instructor and student pilot aboard the single-engine plane, fell into a schoolyard. The accident caused no additional deaths on the ground, but, a short time before, the yard and streets around the school had been full of children.

The National Transportation Safety Board (NTSB), which investigates all public transportation accidents involving the loss of life, stated in its final report that "the probable cause of the accident was the failure of both flight crews to see the other aircraft in sufficient time to initiate evasive action. . . ." The collision took place within the realm and supposed protection of the best the FAA had to offer: the best equipment, the best controllers, and the best procedures. Yet, it is an accident which those facilities and procedures combined to make happen.

The Los Angeles ATIS weather information Delta, being broadcast at the time of the accident, reported 25,000 feet overcast; 40 miles visibility; temperature 60; dew point 19; wind 320 degrees at 7 knots, gusting to 17. Runways 25 Left and Right, and 24 Left at Los Angeles were in use.

At 3:56 P.M. the local controller at Ontario International cleared Golden West 261 for takeoff on Ontario's runway 25 and approved a straight-out departure for the twin-engine plane, since maintaining the runway's 250 degree heading would take it almost directly to Los Angeles International.

With practically no heading change to make, it would be a quick and, for Golden West, economical flight.

Flight 261 maintained its heading and the pilot eased his plane upward in a gradual climb from Ontario's 952-foot elevation to 2,800 feet above sea level.

Nine minutes later, still at 2,800 feet, Golden West 261 flew beneath the 4,000-foot floor of the largest, and highest, tier of the terminal control area (TCA). In another six miles, the floor of the TCA would drop to 2,500 feet, and flight 261 would have to descend or contact Los Angeles approach control for clearance into the TCA.

At 3:46 P.M., exactly ten minutes before Golden West 261 departed Ontario International, a green and white, single-engine Cessna N 11421, based at Long Beach airport eighteen miles southeast of LAX, began its takeoff roll on that airport's runway 25 Right. As with flight 261, Cessna 11421 was cleared for a straight-out departure—to maintain its 250-degree runway heading.

Although straight-out departures aren't standard at most airports, they're not unusual either and are often approved upon the pilot's request. After following the Long Beach local controller's instruction to turn left after crossing the Los Angeles River two miles west of the airport, the Cessna's student pilot, who was accompanied by his instructor, turned northeastward and began climbing toward 2,200 feet.

Since the small training plane routinely stayed well clear of the TCA, it was not equipped with a transponder. By remaining at 2,200 feet, the Cessna would be 300 feet below the 2,500-foot "floor" of the TCA in the area where the student and instructor were flying, possibly en route to El Monte Airport well outside the TCA for practice takeoffs and landings.

At 4:05 P.M., still at 2,800 feet, and still 1,200 feet below the 4,000-foot floor of the TCA at its present location, Golden West flight 261 made its first call to Los Angeles approach control.

"Los Angeles approach, Golden West two sixty-one, Rose Hills (a standard visual reporting point) with Delta."

Will McCloskey, working the Downey radar position made the reply.

"Golden West two sixty-one, squawk zero seven twenty-two and indent. [Pause] Radar contact twenty-three miles east of the [Los Angeles] airport. TCA number two to runway two four Left."

The data block for Golden West's radar target showed the flight level at 2,800 feet, its groundspeed 170 knots.

"Two four left it is, two sixty-one."

The TCA #2 arrival was one of several published arrival procedures for inbound aircraft to follow during good weather. It read:

Enter the TCA at the runway 24 Right localizer ten [mile] DME fix at, and maintain, 1,500 feet until advised by the Los Angeles tower. Contact Los Angeles tower [on] 120.8 at Romeo outer marker (if assigned Runway 24), or 118.9 at Lima outer marker (if assigned runway 25).

Immediately upon receiving the TCA #2 clearance, Golden West departed 2,800 feet.

"*Golden West two sixty-one,*" requested McCloskey as the next sweep of his radar antenna changed the flight's data block to a new reading of 2,600 feet, "*verify leaving two six hundred.*"

"Right on six."

At that moment, 4:06, just two and half minutes before the mid-air collision, Golden West was descending toward 2,200 feet, 300 feet *below* the floor of the TCA which was, in theory at least, specifically established to provide protection from non-transponder-equipped aircraft.

Even if he had considered the TCA protection he was about to relinquish, the pilot of Golden West 261 had other things to think about.

"*Roger* [Golden West 261], *at twelve o'clock five and a half miles is a police helicopter climbing out of one five hundred* (unintelligible) *three thousand VFR. I'll point him out again when he's a little closer. Let me know when you have him in sight.*"

"Two sixty-one, we'll do it."

Traffic at twelve o'clock (straight ahead) is of immediate concern to any pilot. A helicopter, especially hard to see, is an even greater worry. Both pilots of Golden West 261 focused their attention straight ahead, probing the sky for some hint of the police helicopter.

At that moment, 4:08 P.M., at 2,200 feet, 300 feet below the 2,500-foot floor of the TCA which would have excluded the presence of the non-transponder equipped Cessna, Golden West flight 261 and the single-engine plane collided, bringing instant death to fourteen people.

The collision was observed by several witnesses on the ground, and the explosion siezed the attention of many more, but in the Los Angeles TRACON the mid-air collision was silent and, for the moment, unobserved. During the time required for the rotating radar antenna to complete its sweep of the sky, the target and data block of Golden West 261 remained on the radarscope.

Will McCloskey continued issuing advisories to the now deceased pilot of the no-longer-existing airliner.

"Golden West two sixty-one, that helicopter is at eleven-thirty and three miles now. Looks like he's northbound at the moment."

"Golden West two sixty-one," repeated McCloskey, *"that helicopter is now at eleven-thirty and three miles northbound. He's level at three thousand VFR."*

"Golden West two sixty-one?" queried McCloskey.

"Golden West two sixty-one, Los Angeles. If you hear me, ident."

"Golden West two sixty-one, Los Angeles approach control, now do you hear? One, two, three—three, two, one."

As the antenna swept the area where Golden West 261 had been, the radar target and data block representing Golden West 261 were wiped from the radarscope. With the simultaneous loss of radar data and communication, McCloskey knew in his gut that the plane was down; but, functioning partly by training and partly out of hope, he tried to contact the plane once again.

"Golden West two sixty-one, radar contact lost; last position observed seventeen miles east of the Los Angeles Airport. If you hear me, attempt [to] *contact the tower, one two zero point eight."*

He then turned to the approach control team supervisor and told him, "I think I've lost one." He was immediately relieved from his position.

At the A.C.'s desk the watch supervisor immediately began making telephone calls to a list of people and agencies who were to immediately be informed in the event of a suspected crash, mid-air, or other emergency. A few minutes later an incoming call from police confirmed it: Golden West Airlines flight 261 and Cessna N 11421 had collided in midair over Whittier, California.

The wreckage of the twin-engine turbo-prop that had been flight 261 fell into a school yard. The remains of Cessna 11421 had fallen onto the front lawn of a nearby home.

Analysis of the damaged planes revealed that the Cessna struck the left side of the airliner just aft of the cockpit, forward of the larger plane's left wing. The Cessna's instrument panel and firewall were imbedded in the airliner's fuselage, forward of the wing. Propellor slashes made in the Cessna's right wing by the airliner's left engine were at an angle of 88 degrees with the leading edge of the wing. Since the airliner was on a heading of 250 degrees, the angle of impact supported the conclusion that the Cessna was on a northerly heading just prior to impact.

Further study of the wreckage and a computer printout of radar tracking on the airliner indicated that the airliner was to the right and slightly above the Cessna, "masked by the high-wing Cessna's right wing," and that the Cessna was to the left of the airliner, between the airliner and the late afternoon sun, at a time when flight 261's pilots were most probably concentrating their attention straight ahead in an effort to see the police helicopter pointed out to them by the radar approach controller. Flight checks of the location where the collision took place revealed that there was no primary radar coverage in the area when the flight-check aircraft was flown along the presumed flight path of the Cessna.

The NTSB's final report indicated that the inability of the radar to "see" a non-transponder equipped airplane in that location, flying along the presumed course of the Cessna, was due to "tangential effect," meaning that, since the plane was neither getting closer to, nor farther from, the radar antenna, it was invisible to the radar. It was as though the Cessna were flying along the circumference of a circle with the radar at the center.

It was nowhere mentioned in the NTSB's final report that, after establishing the requirement of having a transponder in order for a plane to gain entry to the TCA, the Los Angeles tower worked out letters of agreement with a substantial number of commuter airlines whereby they were to operate *under* the floor of the TCA until reaching its inner core which extends to the ground. The tower chief's letter of agreement had the effect of compressing about fifty flights a day into the narrow space immediately below the floor of the TCA which was already crowded with general aviation planes. The reason given for the tower chief's action was the, "lack of capacity to handle the commuter [airline] traffic within the TCA."

Soon after the mid-air and loss of fourteen lives, Los Angeles' VFR, TCA arrival and departure procedures were quietly changed.

19 Will McCloskey

You spend eight hours a day worked into a chicken-shit frenzy so you can handle whatever is thrown at you. We are not afforded the luxury, when we are presented with a situation, of saying, 'Give me until tomorrow morning to think about it and after staff meeting I'll let you have an answer.' Many times on Downey you'll be handling twenty airplanes at the same time, inbound to Los Angeles.

"IT WAS right after we'd confirmed that Golden West 261 had been involved in the mid-air that the management came in and listened to the tapes of how I'd handled the situation. For days, each day at a higher level, people were going around saying, 'Thank God we're clean; thank God we're clean.' Nobody was saying to me, 'Gee you did a good job, you were handling the traffic exactly the way you were supposed to be doing it.' I spent four days on the witness stand with lawyers coming at me from every angle trying to pin something on me, because, if they could pin something on me, they could go after the FAA. But they couldn't find anything to criticize. If the FAA was 'clean,' it's because I kept them clean. It was like the most important thing to the management was the politics involved—being 'clean.'

"You are working under tremendous pressure. Failure to call a pilot's attention to possibly conflicting traffic can be fatal. Failure to make sure an instruction is acknowledged can be fatal. Failure to make the proper call, or simply transposing two simple numbers, can be fatal.

"You can't see it if you come into a facility and stand behind a controller, but one of the greatest hazards to the flying public is the schedule we have to work. You work two days of days; then two days on the swing shift; and then one mid-watch, eleven at night to seven in the morning. Your body never has time to adjust to that. You have to eat and sleep and work at constantly changing times of the day, and nobody in your family can have a normal social life. The quick-turn-around, mid-watch schedule doesn't even allow you to get 8 hours sleep. You get off at three in the afternoon and you're back working traffic at eleven o'clock that night. Most airlines won't allow their pilots to fly unless they've had at least 2 hours off for every hour they've flown. And the maximum any airline pilot flies in any one month is 85 hours. We regularly work 120 hours a month and often have to work additional overtime.

"The rotating shift schedule is totally against what society has programmed for a family unit. Your children's school is geared to society's schedule, so is your wife's job if she has one, so are weekend social activities, so is television and the times that stores are open. So your wife is frustrated because she can't have a meaningful job; your kids come crashing into the house from school when you're trying to sleep; and, if you have to do some shopping or need to have the car worked on, half the time you do those things during the eight hours *after* you sleep and the other half of the time you have to do those things the eight hours *before* you sleep. The two, two, and one schedule produces a stressful marriage relationship and makes for problems between you and your kids. The public should realize that, when I have these problems at home, I *might* take them to work with me.

"It's important to me to have somebody who can either listen or talk when I get home and who knows that's what I expect. I don't always have to come home and rant and rave, and I don't always have to come home and go into the garage and hide. I come in and sit down and the first thing I say is, 'How was your day?', and that's an opener for both of us. Either one of us can drop it, or we can take it and run. We can communicate but we don't feel there's any set way we have to communicate. Connie is a nurse and she's worked with cancer patients for years and there are lots of times when she gets home and doesn't want to talk or hear anyone's problems; so she understands what I feel and doesn't meet me at the door with her hair up in curlers and the fact that Blair shit in his pants today or that one of the kids beat up on the little girl next door. In our marriage, because of the job stress and the hours I have to work, we both try a lot harder. Right after we got married Connie went through private-pilot ground school and she's been to work with me. A lot of times things happen at work which I can't explain to Connie because it's not possible for her to understand, but I know she *wants* to understand and, even if I end up not talking about it, knowing she's interested helps.

"Next to our insane work schedule, I'd have to say that controllers having to train new people is perhaps the next most hazardous condition affecting the flying public. We frequently have near mid-airs, and almost near mid-airs, during training. I'm not a trained teacher; I'm a controller and that's what I do best. But if you are a controller you have to train people whether you're suited for it or not. It's part of your duties. Except for a short course at the FAA academy in Oklahoma when you first come to work for the FAA, controller training isn't done by professional instructors. We need professionals who must also be very good controllers, and they must be compensated for it.

"A person with a bachelor's degree can't just go out and teach. He has to have credentials. It should be the same in the FAA. We're talking about more than just shaping minds; we're talking about shaping bodies—from a comfortable shape in an airline seat into a mangled mess on the ground. Going through the training program at a new facility is a real pain. It's humiliating, mentally exhausting, physically tiring, and emotionally draining. When you have a wrung-out trainee on a busy position with a controller who isn't at all suited to instructing, you're asking for a deal. When the trainee's working the position you have to allow the situation to get worse than you ordinarily would to see if he'll recognize the situation and be able to correct it. You might be dying to say something but you can't, because, if you do, how will you ever know what that trainee might or might not do after you turn him loose on the position with people's lives involved?

"Since the FAA started its 'affirmative action program' to bring in minorities, it seems that standards have been lowered so far that things could be getting unsafe. I am working with one of these trainees right now. Julia is not now, and never will be, a good controller. She might at some point in time be able to hack her way through it, but she is not the kind of person we need at Los Angeles. One problem that I have with her is that she seems to consider her race above all other things. Anything I say to her she takes as a reflection on her being black. She has that attitude completely, no matter what is said. She has accused me and other controllers of being chauvinistic, saying we don't think women should be controllers. Although I don't necessarily think that women should be controllers, I don't think they shouldn't be. Why not? One of the three best controllers in Los Angeles tower is a woman, Pat Hammond. And the FAA has some very sharp black woman controllers; Katie Harper, now in Longview, Texas, is one who comes to mind.

"When I'm working with a controller what I look at is, can they produce? That's all I care about. If something comes up and Julia can't handle it, she just ignores it. Every airliner that's going to depart Los Angeles needs an IFR (instrument flight rules) clearance outlining its route, altitude, and so on. Each pilot contacts clearance delivery for his clearance and if she's hassled Julia just doesn't answer the phone. I've had to tell her, 'Look, it's just like when you're calling somebody on the telephone. If you know they're there, you're going to let that phone ring until they answer. Now, those pilots who call for clearance, they know you're here and they're going to keep calling until *you* answer. They don't want any excuses. They don't care if you are having problems or if the computer is behind, they are going to keep calling until you give them their clearance or you assure them you are working on it.' When she does respond, Julia will just pick out someone at random and ignore the others. Pretty soon she's fifteen minutes behind and it gets to the point of delaying an aircraft. Delays mean money, and any time money is involved the Air Transport Association comes down on the FAA and the local region comes down on the controller—not the trainee but the controller who's trying to conduct the training.

"One afternoon right in the middle of the arrival rush Julia was training on ground control—airplanes moving all over the place, or trying to—and she just unplugged her headset, said 'I don't want to do this no more,' and walked off the position. Steve Wilkins was training her then and he had to really move fast to keep things from falling apart. He couldn't even follow her to find out what was the matter.

"Julia can quote the manual to you, but she can't use it and can't translate it into practice. So far we must have given her three or four times the amount of hours anyone else would be allowed. She hasn't made it yet; I don't think she ever will, but the management is bound and determined she's going to get checked out.

"If she ever is certified I'd sure as hell never fly in or out of Los Angeles while she's working the traffic. No way.

"Part of the training problem we have at Los Angeles you probably don't find at less busy places because LAX is a strong attraction to a lot of controllers. There are three strong reasons why controllers come here. One is money; LAX pays more than a less busy facility. Two is that it's a stepping stone into management—and people who want to be managers aren't always the best controllers. Three is prestige; there is a vast amount of prestige connected with working in the TRACON or tower at Los Angeles. Nothing in the FAA western region approaches the status of working here.

"There are an awful lot of controllers here, maybe even most of us, for the status."

20 Departure One

No matter how heavy or light the traffic is, the guys are always needling each other. Everything you do or say here is heard by the guys around you—and seen on radar. If you fuck up, everybody's going to jump on you and kid you about it. There's a pecking order here and everybody knows pretty much where they stand. Being new, you know where you stand—at the bottom.

IF YOU wash out in the TRACON, you'll wash out on Downey. A beginner in the TRACON—new to Los Angeles and fresh from your last assignment at Detroit or Denver or Phoenix or Minneapolis or Miami—you have to memorize radio frequencies, reporting points, standard arrival routes (STARs), and standard instrument departures (SIDs); you have to draw and label maps and charts and diagrams until you can do it in your sleep; and, after you've spent weeks in the TRACON and control tower for familiarization, then you can begin in departure control.

The training program says you'll begin as departure hand-off controller. You won't be allowed to talk to airplanes. Although you may have been the sharpest radar controller there ever was where you came from, it doesn't count for much here. Here is different and you're a trainee. And a trainee is someone that nobody trusts—because you might unknowingly set up a deal someone else will hang for. You begin by handling paper (flight progress strips) and by using the telephone, the keyboard computer terminal in front of you just to the right of the radar, and the trackball, which you share with the radar controller who's seated at your left in front of the position's radarscope, in order to coordinate departures from LAX and several nearby airports. If you've had prior FAA radar experience, the training program allows you 35 hours to become proficient on departure hand-off—compared to 125 hours on the departure radar controller position—and 200 hours on arrival radar where you'll be running the show on Downey or Stadium.

Working departure one, you and your radar-controller partner are responsible for a large sector of airspace within a twenty-mile radius of LAX which, on the face of a clock, would extend from 8:30 (almost due west of the airport) counter-clockwise to almost 4:00. It's the largest single piece of the airspace pie which surrounds LAX. In most areas of the sector, you "own" from the surface to 6,000 feet. Every plane departing LAX will be handed off by the tower to one of the two departure control positions. Any pilot who will be flying south of LAX will be told by the tower to contact the departure one radar controller, *"PSA five forty-six* (he's going to San Diego), *contact departure now, one two four point three."*

"Los Angeles departure, PSA five forty-six with you out of one thousand."

The controller's response usually includes one of the several standard routings between LAX and San Diego.

"Roger, PSA five forty-six, radar contact; cleared to the San Diego airport via direct Seal Beach VORTAC, Victor [airway] *two three* [to the] *Oceanside VORTAC; maintain five thousand."*

Before PSA 546 reaches the limit of your airspace, you will use the trackball to slew your position's symbol, an "S" on the radarscope, so that it's superimposed on the target representing

PSA 546. As you press the "enter" key on your computer keyboard, PSA 546's data block begins to blink as it moves onto the radarscope of the TRACON south of LAX whose airspace is tangent to yours. When the hand-off controller for that airspace accepts the responsibility for PSA 546, the data block will change from blinking to steady on his radarscope—and will vanish from yours.

Now, at 7:00 P.M., less than thirty planes an hour are taking off from LAX; figuring half of those for departure one, it averages out to just one plane every four minutes for the position you're working. The pace is slower now than at any time since you came on duty at 3:00 P.M. Departure one and two were pumping out more than fifty planes an hour then, not a peak for the day, but close to it. There's time to loosen up now and come down a bit from the late afternoon rush.

"Hey," the controller acting as team coordinator asks, "do you know why they have that big hump over the cockpit on the 747?"

"No," you answer, knowing you're in for something. "Why?"

"So there's enough headroom for those $100,000-a-year pilots to sit on their wallets."

"Departure, American four twenty-seven with you outta nine-hundred," calls the pilot of a San Diego–bound 727, saving you from having to laugh.

"American four twenty-seven, Los Angeles Departure, radar contact," replies your partner seated before the radarscope; *"after passing the VOR* (radio navigational station), *turn left heading two one zero degrees."*

"O.K., American four twenty-seven."

In a few minutes you'll be handing 427 off to Coast TRACON.

"Hey," says someone, "were any of you guys around here when those four Japan Airlines pilots came in here the other day? Man, they were so short I swear they must have been pilot and pilot, and co-pilot and co-pilot. I figure flyin' those 747s they got, one of 'em must have sat in each seat plus one each down there on the floor workin' the rudder pedals."

"Cessna twenty-six Sierra," says the radar controller to a private plane he's been watching on the radar, *"traffic one o'clock, five miles* [is] *westbound, same direction; traffic one o'clock, ten miles southeast-bound, is a United jet inbound—will be above you. Contact Los Angeles center now, one three five point five."*

"Twenty-six Sierra, wilco and we got the jet in sight above us."

"Golden West eight fifty-one, you're now at Hermosa, contact Coast departures on one two seven point two."

You slew to Golden West 851's radar target and press the "enter" key above your trackball. Eight fifty-one's data block begins to blink.

"Hey, buddy," says the radar man at your side, "you should've seen that one comin' up 'cause he was gettin' close to Coast's airspace. You got it in time though; just stay on top, that's all."

You catch American 427 just about to penetrate Coast TRACON's airspace. Quick! Slew, hit "enter" above the trackball. Blink-blink-blink, goes 427's data block just in time. You made it.

"Don't forget him now; make sure Coast accepts;" blink-blink —gone! Coast has him.

"So I took this teacup," the team supervisor, the TRACON's professional Irishman, is saying, "and I carefully stuffed it with tissue paper. Then I wrapped it up in my brand new cashmere sweater, see. Then I put it in my suitcase surrounded by all my clothes, because, you know, it's very old and valuable. Well, when I got back here and got off the plane from Ireland and I opened my suitcase for customs, the damn thing was broken. TWA broke that teacup into a million pieces. And it was my sainted grandmother's teacup! I'll tell you guys one thing; I ain't ever gonna let TWA forget that one. Any time I'm workin' traffic and I got a TWA, they're gonna pay me just a little bit more for breakin' that teacup. If I live long enough that's gonna be a hundred-thousand-dollar teacup, believe me! On my grandmother's grave it is!"

"Hey, Strother, you're safe now; I'm back!" calls one of the team supervisors returning from his brown bag dinner in the ready-room.

"The only time we're safe around here is when you're gone, you turkey!" somebody says.

"Departure, United seventy-seven with you; we're leaving one thousand for eleven thousand."

"United seventy-seven, Los Angeles departure, radar contact, after the shoreline, turn left heading two one zero."

"Left to two one zero at the shoreline, United seventy-seven."

Looking at the flight strip you see that United 77's headed for San Diego just a few miles south of LAX. In a few minutes you'll be handing him off to Coast TRACON; slew, "enter," blink-blink; nothing to it!

"United seventy-seven, turn left to one six zero," says the radar controller as he vectors the United jet away from an inbound plane.

"Left to one six zero, United seventy-seven."

Over at the assistant chief's desk someone momentarily turns up the monitor speaker to check the ATIS broadcast, ". . . two thousand, two-hundred scattered, three thousand five-hundred overcast, visibility ten, temperature six-three, wind two four zero at eleven, altimeter two-nine point eight seven, simultaneous instrument approaches in progress, runways two-five Right and two-four Left. Inform the approach controller on initial contact that you have arrival information November. Los Angeles arrival information November. Two thousand, two-hundred sca——."

"Hey, Charlie," someone calls to the controller just turning off the speaker, "You ain't planning on sneaking out early are you?"

"Naw," says someone else, "he was just checkin' the weather because he was curious—weren't you Charlie?"

"Hey, why don't you bastards fuck off?" says Charlie heading out the door toward the ready-room coffee machine to fill his cup before relieving another controller.

"United seventy-seven, contact Los Angeles Center now, one three two point eight five."

You roll the trackball in its socket, slewing your position's symbol to United 77's target. You hit the trackball's "enter" key; blink-blink-blink—now the data block's gone, the hand-off accepted by the center. You note the hand-off time on United 77's flight strip and set it aside to be included with others for the position's total traffic count when your watch ends at 11:00 P.M.

"Los Angeles departure, Golden West seven fifty-six with you climbing to five."

"Golden West seven fifty-six, radar contact, turn left zero nine zero and intercept the Los Angeles one two three radial; resume normal navigation."

"Left to zero nine zero, normal nav, Golden West seven fifty-six."

Golden West's bright radar target begins its turn away from the plane's original 250-degree runway heading, a left, almost complete U-turn until it's heading due east. The data block follows, attached by a one-inch "leader line" on the scope. It's like a luminous lime-green, square balloon being pulled around by a kid running on a playground. You try to imagine what would happen if two leader lines got tangled up there—even though the planes didn't touch. Would they come falling to the ground in a tangled confusion?

Center will have to turn 756 soon after they get him; he's bound for Salt Lake City and you don't get there by heading due east from Los Angeles.

"Departure, Continental two fifty-six, we're out of seven hundred feet for two three zero [23,000 feet]."

"Continental two fifty-six, Los Angeles departure, radar contact."

Coast TRACON calls you on the interphone. They see Golden West headed toward their airspace and have numerous military planes on their radar at 5,000 so they ask you to hold Golden West 756 at 4,000 for the hand-off. You confirm you'll do it and advise the departure one radar controller.

"Golden West seven fifty-six," he says, *"maintain four thousand."*

"Roger, seven fifty-six."

"Golden West seven fifty-six, contact Coast departure now one two seven point two. So long."

"So long, seven fifty-six."

You slew to 756's radar target, hit "enter"; blink-blink—gone. Ho-hum.

"Continental two fifty-six, turn left heading two zero zero."

"Heading two zero zero for Continental two fifty-six."

"Continental two fifty-six, maintain three five hundred; proceed direct to Seal Beach."

"Two fifty-six."

"Continental two fifty-six, contact Los Angeles Center one three two point eight five."

Slew, "enter," blink. Yawn. Note hand-off time on the four-by-one-inch, light green "shortie" flight strip. Put it in the stack for later count. Ho-hum.

"Hey, Sammy," one of the controllers on coffee break asks the departure two controller seated to your right, "where'd you get the new toupé?"

"Oh," he answers matter-of-factly, "at the same place where I take my kid to get his hair cut. They handle hairpieces there too —it's an Italian place—that's where the best hair comes from."

"Yeah, they also teach you how to walk with a swish—right?"

"No, but I learned how to talk with my hands better!"

"Los Angeles, Golden West eight fifty-one with you, climbing to five."

"Golden West eight fifty-one, Los Angeles departure, radar contact, turn left one six zero."

"Left one six zero for Golden West eight fifty-one."

"Say present altitude, Golden West eight fifty-one."

"Just outta eight hundred feet, eight fifty-one."

"Working departure hand-off's not too bad," remarks the radar-controller–instructor you're assigned to, "but arrival hand-off will be a lot different. If you're a fairly new hand-off man, chances are you're not going to have the coordinated inbound planes' speed [for spacing] with the center the way an experienced man will. You'll have to learn the radar position before you'll be able to anticipate what [speeds] the radar controller will need [in order to be able to work in his other traffic]."

"If you're a *great* hand-off man, you'll never take an airplane unless you know where you would put that airplane. The radar controller you're working with might not do it that way, but at least you, in your own mind, should have a spot for that airplane if he were to drop dead in ten seconds. Not only that, you have to make sure that by accepting a plane you're not handing the radar man an unsolvable problem. Each time you accept a hand-off, you need to have said to yourself, 'I could handle that plane if I were working the radar position—I'd know where to put that guy.'

"What the radar man can accomplish on Downey or Stadium is directly proportional to how much the hand-off man can accomplish in setting up speed control with center and also, to a lesser extent, how much faith he has in the radar man. If you're working Downey hand-off, you conduct yourself according to who's working the radar position. If he's a recently checked out guy, you don't load him up. If it's somebody you've worked with for years, you can give him more airplanes because you know he can handle it."

The best lessons are sometimes taught in the least expected places. You'll remember this guy in your prayers.

"Golden West eight fifty-one, turn further left to zero seven zero. This will be a vector [away from other aircraft] *for spacing."*

"O.K., zero seven zero for vector, eight fifty-one."

"Departure, Western twenty-nine zero five, we're out of five hundred feet now, climbing to two three zero."

"Western twenty-nine zero five, Los Angeles departure, radar contact, maintain six thousand."

"Maintain six for Western twenty-nine zero five."

"Western twenty-nine zero five, turn right, heading two seven zero."

"Two seven zero for twenty-nine zero five, roger."

"Departure, Continental seventy-six seventy-nine with you. Through one five hundred for two three zero."

"Continental seventy-six seventy-nine, Los Angeles departure,

radar contact, turn left, heading two one zero. When you leave four thousand proceed direct [to] *Seal Beach."*

"Left to two one zero, outta four direct to Seal Beach, Continental seventy-six seventy-nine."

"Golden West eight fifty-one, turn right now, heading one four zero and intercept the Los Angeles one two three [degree] *radial; resume normal navigation."*

"Roger, Golden West eight fifty-one."

"Golden West eight fifty-one, traffic nine o'clock and a mile; appears to be a departure from Hawthorne."

"Golden West eight fifty-one, no contact."

If the plane departing Hawthorne had been an IFR flight you'd have received its flight plan from center and passed it along to Hawthorne tower; so you'd have known who it was. Or, if the pilot had been northbound into the TCA, he'd have called departure one for entry clearance. But, since he's operating under visual flight rules and southbound away from the TCA, there's no need for him to contact anyone after taking off.

"Golden West eight fifty-one, contact Coast departure now, one two seven point two."

"So long, eight fifty-one."

Slew, "enter," blink-blink; you note the hand-off time on 851's flight strip. "Keep 'em comin' you bastards," you say to yourself; "tonight I'm so hot I can handle anything!"

"Departure, Western six thirty-one's outta six zero zero now for two three zero."

"Western six thirty-one, Los Angeles departure, radar contact. After passing the VOR turn left, heading two one zero."

"Left to two one zero over the VOR, Western six thirty-one."

You look at 631's flight strip. He's headed for Phoenix. You wonder if you should have bid for an opening there. You wonder what it would be like. "Naw," you finally tell yourself, "LAX is it. Make it here and you can have anyplace you want."

"Continental seventy-six seventy-nine, contact Los Angeles center one three two point eight five. So long."

Slew, "enter," blink-blink-blink-blink-blink-blink-blink-blink-blink—"Hey," you wonder, "what's with that center controller; he's not accepting the hand-off." Blink-blink-blink—gone. You ask the radar controller, "I wonder why that was?"

"Nothing," he tells you, "probably scratchin' his ass. It happens though; you just gotta watch them until you see center take the hand-off. When you're really pumpin' out the airplanes you gotta make sure you don't just initiate the hand-off and forget it. We've had a couple of deals that way: hand-off man not getting the confirmation and the center controller busy with some problem, not seeing whoever it was you're trying to hand off."

"Western six thirty-one, when you leave four thousand proceed direct to Seal Beach."

[Silence]

"Western six thirty-one, when you leave four thousand proceed direct to Seal Beach."

"Direct outta four, Western six thirty-one."

"Los Angeles departure, PSA seven twenty-three's outta one thousand for two thousand."

"PSA seven twenty-three, Los Angeles departure, radar contact. Maintain three thousand; expect higher in three miles. Traffic ter o'clock, two miles northbound at four thousand."

"Maintain three thousand, PSA seven twenty-three."

"That's odd," you comment to yourself, "seven twenty-three's headed for Sacramento. Wonder why he didn't go off two four Left?"

"Western six thirty-one, contact Los Angeles center now, one three two point eight five."

"Western six thirty-one."

Slew, "enter," blink-blink—gone. You write 631's hand-off time on the flight strip. "Christ!" you kid yourself, "beautiful, just beautiful! Boy, I'm really cookin' tonight!" But you keep a straight face.

"PSA seven twenty-three, climb and maintain flight level two three zero [23,000 feet]."

"Maintain two three zero, PSA seven twenty-three."

"Departure, Western seventy-six climbing to two thousand."

"Western seventy-six, Los Angeles departure, radar contact, climb and maintain flight level two three zero."

"Roger, flight level two three zero now, Western seventy-six."

"PSA seven twenty-three, contact Los Angeles Center now, one three five point five."

So that's how he handles it; PSA 723 off 25 Right and then far enough west and high enough so that he's outside departure two's and Stadium's airspace before he's handed off to the center and turned northbound.

Slew, "enter," blink-blink-blink—gone. Hand-off time on the flight strip.

"Hey, you two," says the team supervisor, "why don't you go have dinner; you're relieved."

"You want to relieve me," says the departure one radar controller as the two of you relinquish your chairs, "you can't relieve me! I'm relieved when you go home, you fucker."

You wait as the radar controller briefs the one controller who relieved the two of you, then you both head for the ready-room and the brown bags in your tiny lockers.

"Western seventy-six," says the new departure one controller, apparently sure who the plane's pilot is, *"verify you're over your present position now."*

"Well, I was a minute ago, but I ain't now," answers Western 76.

The ready-room, as you look around while having your dinner of two sandwiches and an apple, isn't much: maybe twenty by twenty feet, four well-worn, formica-top tables and a score of straight back chairs with padded seats and truck-stop chrome. Along two of the walls there are banks of tiny, twelve-inch-by-twelve-inch lockers.

To the left of the door there's a candy machine: Hershey bars, M & M's, "Creme" sugar wafers (yuck!), Double Nut Bars, Snickers, Planter's Peanuts, Smokehouse Almonds, and "Van" cookies.

The soft drink machine to the right of the candy machine dispenses Coca-Cola, Tab, ginger ale, and wild cherry.

The TV set in the corner is turned on. Angie Dickenson is playing *Police Woman,* standing there holding her purse while two big cops are trying to break down a door. They run full tilt into it; crash! Nothing happens. Angie Dickenson bites her lower lip. Crash! The door gives a little. Maybe she'll take out her pistol and shoot the lock off. Whoever was in that room is either dead or out the window by now. Crash!

There's a tall, gold golf trophy up there on a shelf to the left of the TV set. The trophy's being ridden by a stuffed "Snoopy" with his flying helmet and goggles on. In the corner there's a medium-sized refrigerator and an infrared oven for heating sandwiches. On the wall to the left of the TV there's a green chalk board for training. On another wall, to the right, there's a glass-covered bulletin board with FAA and union notices.

There's an FAA notice telling you that the per diem subsistence rate for temporary duty in Manhattan, the Bronx, or Staten Island is $50.00 per day, but that if you're in Brooklyn or Queens you'll only get $39.00 a day. Doing time within the corporate limits of San Francisco and/or Oakland will net you $39.00 a day; and each day in Boston will get you $38.00.

There is a memo titled *Working Environment Improvement Through Idea Exchanges.* It goes on for a full page and is signed; Frank Happy, Chief, Air Traffic Division.

And there's the typical bulletin board stuff:

FOR SALE
GE Air Conditioner, Room Type: 6,000 BTU.
Fits sliding window. Call J.R., LAX tower.

FOR SALE
1974 Zenith Chromacolor 25" console TV.
"Avanti" model, white top, sides and base with
rosewood. Sold new for $699.00. Will sell for
$470.00. Call Ballantyne, LAX TRACON.

And the not-too-typical:

Carl Rice 40, ATCS, Fresno Air Terminal, Fresno, California, died of a heart attack May 1, 1978. He is survived by his wife, one son, and one daughter.

[Signed] Glyndon M. Riley
Chairman, Voluntary Pledge Plan

There *was* somebody still in that room when Angie Dickenson finally got in there. The two big cops have him in handcuffs now and somebody's telling the policewoman what a terriffic job she just did.

Time to get back to work. Maybe they'll let you work a little radar.

"Hey, glad to see you made it back!" says the team supervisor. "How about you relieve Jimmy over there on departure two hand-off for a while."

Two hours of departure two hand-off and it's time to go home. Stepping outside into the cool, damp night air you can see the visibility's even less than reported by the ATIS. The base of the clouds is lower too; it's less than 1,000 feet overcast.

"Looks like about 900 overcoats," remarks one of the controllers, glancing up at the bottom of the cloud layer as he steps through the door with you.

If you do wash out in the TRACON, you realize as you walk through the mist toward your dew-covered car, it won't be Downey that finally gets you.

21

The Miami Hotshot

Make 'em work for you. If you can get the pilots to work for you, you can do anything with them—and that's a true statement. As long as you can get them to work for you and make it sound as though they're doing you the biggest favor in the world to fly that airplane, you can do anything you want and they'll love every minute of it.

RICH DOLECKI —"Dildo" to controllers at the TRACON—is new to Los Angeles. He's maybe five feet six inches, and about the right weight for his height. At twenty-nine, his brown hair is just long enough for some dark-suited business-man in a four-door sedan stopped next to Dolecki's motorcycle at a traffic light to glance over at him and think, "No-good, smart-ass kid!"

He came to LAX straight from Miami TRACON. It was a transfer at his request: no FAA moving allowance and, since his pay grade was already the same as LAX TRACON's, no salary increase even if he did make it in Los Angeles. Like other controll-ers here, he wanted to see if he had what it takes. He does. He was signed-off on every one of the TRACON's controller positions in about two-thirds the time most people require.

"It doesn't make any difference where you come from. It could be O'Hare or JFK," Dolecki explains, "you still have to prove yourself here. You don't just have to prove you can work the traffic, you have to prove it with a man standing behind you who's listening to every word you say and who demands that you be letter-perfect in everything. Not only does your job performance have to be adequate, but you have to perform to the taste of the man watching you because he's told you how he wants it. So you have to work the traffic his way—use some of the things he would use because you've got to perform in a way that will please him. It makes the job doubly hard because he's watching your traffic and listening to you on his headset and he's saying 'Why didn't you do it this way?' and 'Why didn't you do it that way?' and all the time you're trying to answer him and you're still working the traffic. Actually, it's easier when traffic is very, very busy because then he can only catch so many things. When it's all over all he remembers is that you moved the airplanes and he forgets all the little picky things he might have called you on.

"When I came here from Miami I was cocky, up to a point, because I'd been at a busy facility. I know how the traffic has to move and I can do it; so when I came to LAX I had problems. Everybody tried to take their shots at me because they thought, 'The kid came from Miami and he's already the same pay grade we are so we'll just show him he really wasn't where the traffic is.'

"Nobody works Downey radar for more than an hour, yet they'd put me on there during the arrival rush and leave me on there two hours. When Downey was slow I wouldn't be on the position, and when it was busy I'd be in there. After you've been on that position about two hours you feel like taking a long nap someplace because you're really totally exhausted.

"Miami had a lot more sectors than LAX. We ran basically the same amount of traffic, but we were working with nine radar positions there compared to four radar positions here. And you don't have any airspace at Los Angeles; there's just no place you can turn an airplane when you get into a bad situation. At Miami you had a lot of airspace and if speed control didn't work you could use [diverging heading] vectors for separation. If something happens here and you have to turn an airplane to get him outta there, you have to use your hand-off man to coordinate with somebody to use their airspace; so you work terribly hard to keep things under control so you can stay in your own airspace. It's much, much more difficult at LAX than I really understood when I first got here. There's a lot to it.

"You've normally got four air traffic separation tools you can use: heading, altitude, time, and speed. Working Downey and Stadium, about the only thing you've got is speed control. You've got no airspace to turn anybody into, so you can't use *headings*. They're all headed for the runway following the same glide path, so there goes *altitude* out the window. They're landing almost one a minute during the arrival rush, so you can't use *time*. The only thing you've got left to work with is *speed control,* and you've got to get everybody's cooperation or it won't work.

"When I first went through training in Las Vegas I had an older instructor who is probably one of the greatest things that ever happened to me because his first phrase was, 'Make 'em work for you.' When it's busy and you've got your inbounds strung out five miles apart for fifty or sixty miles, you're adjusting speed to maintain that. You've got to have a minimum of five miles separation outside the outer marker, and four miles passing the marker at 160 knots to have three miles separation as they're crossing the fence. Less separation than that and the tower will have to send them around. If I assign a speed, I can use a phrase out of the book, 'Reduce speed to one six zero knots.' O.K., that's clear and it's concise, but there's no life to it; there's no voice inflection. Or else I can come up and say, 'Can you reduce speed to one six zero for me?' You make it sound like he's doing you a favor, which in a way he is, and he comes back and says, 'Sure, we can do that.' Then if you need it you can say, 'If feasible, can you reduce speed to one four zero knots for me? I really need it, I got traffic ahead of you that's dying,' and he says, 'Sure, we can do that for you.' But if you use the book phrase and say, 'If feasible reduce speed to one four zero knots,' he's going to say, 'Stick it up your ass, partner; we can't fly this airplane that slow.'

"When you use the same voice, when you use phrases right out of the book, it doesn't arouse them at all—doesn't give them any excitement—nothing! So you make 'em work for you—and they love every minute of it. It's back to the old thing; you treat people basically the way you want to be treated. If you do that, you're going to get things your way. Some of these old-timer airline captains never learn that. They come up on the frequency and say, 'I want this,' or 'I want that,' like it's a demand, and you don't feel like helping them. But when a pilot comes up and says, 'Approach, we're running a little late and we'd appreciate direct Lima as soon as convenient,' you'll bust your ass to give it to him and maybe even build him a nice hole so you can turn him in [to the runway] quicker. When a pilot comes up and says, 'I'd like this,' or 'I'd like that,' I'll do it for him if I can. It makes me feel good.

"You've got to have cooperation from the Stadium man too. You're building holes in the string of inbounds for Stadium's traffic. If the Stadium man misses one hole you can understand that, but if he misses two or three you start to get a little bit irritated and you just hope he gets off the position. Everybody will have a bad day now and then, but it complicates things when they do. There isn't any room for bad days.

"Stadium has a problem when there's good visibility because their traffic eastbound over Santa Monica is cleared for a visual approach and pilots make that right U-turn inbound when they feel they're ready to. They'll overshoot the airport every time. They'll be sitting there at 2,000 feet looking straight down at the end of the runway.

"The other day the tower asked a visual that looked pretty high for 24 Left, 'Are you sure you're going to be able to get it down O.K.?' and the pilot answered back, 'I ain't ever left one up here yet,' but he still had to go around. I don't know what they tell the passengers.

"The worst weather though, is when the visibility's good

enough for them to see each other, but not good enough so you can use visual separation all the way to the airport. Most of the time the visibility's so bad they can't see each other; on a day when a pilot finally can see the other aircraft, since it's unusual for him to see so many planes, he gets nervous. When a pilot can't see the other planes, you give him an airspeed to maintain which you know is going to provide the separation you want. But when the visibility's better than usual, and a pilot sees that airplane in front of him or beside him, he starts slowing down—starts using his own speed instead of what you gave him. Generally they think they're a lot closer than they actually are, so they'll bleed off speed and they'll be slowed down to maybe 140 knots. If you've got fifteen airplanes in trail slowed down to 140 it's an impossible situation because they can't fly much slower than that. Now you can't build any holes for Stadium or your traffic coming up from the south. So what are you going to do? You have to pull a few out of there, keep 'em on runway heading and hold them at 2,000 feet until they're out over the ocean and then hand them off to Stadium and let him bring them back in again. Or you'll turn them south and then bring them back north to work them in the best you can with your inbounds from south of the airport. You get phone calls from pilots when they have to go around, but they bring it on themselves by ignoring your speed control. Too much visibility can be a pain.

"When the visibility's really down and we're really loaded, the A.C. will call for parallel approaches, but nobody likes to do that because it takes two extra controllers to monitor parallels and we're not staffed for that. So that means you lose your coordinator or somebody has to work without a hand-off man. Since we're short-handed anyway, you'll also probably end up eating your dinner at the position.

"Right now I'm thriving on the stress, but I'm twenty-nine. When you get older, around thirty-five, your thoughts aren't as quick as they once were. If I stay here and build up some time I can go on experience for a while when I'm older, but not for long because everything is always changing. By the time I'm forty I'll be burned out, but I can't see myself as chief in a little tower somewhere. I'm the kind of person who needs a challenge. What I do now is get off by myself as much as I can. I've got a motorcycle and a lot of times on my days off I'll go to Las Vegas, but the main reason is just to be alone. I tell Ruth [my wife] I'm going. She doesn't like it, but she understands it. I guess I'm being a little bit selfish. I guess if Ruth wanted to get away it would be fine if we had someone to watch the kid while I'm at work. If it was on my days off that she wanted to get away I'd probably say it was O.K. I'd be reluctant, but I'd do it. I know the job is tough on my marriage. Somebody told me controllers have twice the national average divorce rate and more heart attacks and ulcers. If the job doesn't kill you all at once it gets you by attrition. But while you're doing it, it's an unbelievable feeling of satisfaction. You feel you're the biggest person in the world."

22   Some Airlines Are More Equal Than Others

The Eastern flight broke out of the overcast fifteen hundred feet above the ground right over the middle of the runway, too high to land and not enough fuel to make a circuit back through the terminal control area; so he made a left 360-degree turn and violated Hughes Airport. They had traffic on final at Hughes. He also just missed a couple of planes we had on final which we had to pull out of his way. A comedy of errors. We found out he was low on fuel and didn't want to tell anybody because he didn't want anyone to know about his horrible planning. He almost killed himself and some other people.

TOO OFTEN, the relationships between controllers and airline pilots in high-density areas is one of begrudging trust, born not of confidence and mutual respect, but of regulation and necessity. Controllers make mistakes; so do pilots. When controllers make theirs, it's in front of co-workers who good-naturedly make sure they don't forget they're only human. Often the knowledge of a pilot's poor procedures or faulty flying remains confined to the sanctum of the flight deck.

During the months I spent living and working with controllers in Los Angeles, I came to feel that, on the face of it at least, controllers seem to know more about flying an airplane than airline pilots know about air traffic control. *Obviously* a jet airliner has thousands of switches, dials, controls, and circuit breakers; and *obviously* the captain's life, and the lives of his passengers and crew are at stake. And it is true, as one airline pilot stated to the FAA, that, "Not one air traffic controller ever died falling from his chair." Yet an approach controller in a high-density area will often be working twenty to twenty-five planes at the same time, all moving in a relatively small airspace at hundreds of miles an hour. Multiply twenty planes by 200 passengers per aircraft and you're sitting there at your radar with 4,000 lives in your hands. Although it's true, almost, that no air traffic controller ever died in his chair, the heart attack rate for controllers is six times greater than the heart attack rate for pilots.

Fortunately for the smooth operation of the air traffic system, about 40 percent of controllers are pilots. Several score are former jet-qualified airline pilots who tired of the airlines' on-again, off-again unpaid furloughs and returned to their previous employment—as air traffic controllers. Many other controllers, former military fliers and active armed forces reserve and National Guard pilots, are quite at home flying heavy, multi-engine jet aircraft. Their knowledge of the problems faced by pilots and of the capabilities and limitations of large jet aircraft enables them to make the system operate more safely than otherwise might be possible.

An agreement between the FAA and most every United States airline provides for occasional controller familiarization flights in the cockpits of scheduled airliners. Admittedly, *fam* flights are an interesting change in controllers' normal routine, but they are also a valuable opportunity for gaining additional knowledge which controllers don't overlook. Although pilots are welcome at airport control towers, radar rooms, and en route centers, we saw not one United States airline pilot at any air traffic facility during our six months of research for this book—and neither did any controller we spoke to. "You fairly often get the foreign airline pilots," we were told, "and the private pilots and corporate jet pilots, but we hardly ever see a United States airline pilot here. I guess they figure they know all there is to know."

If controllers were running the FAA, they might require airline pilots to spend a certain amount of time at the air traffic facilities of each of the major terminals they regularly fly into. It might perhaps be done on a one-time basis coincident with airport familiarization flights which are part of every captain's route certification. It might lead to a better understanding of air traffic control and reduce some of the on-the-air bickering that sometimes goes on between pilots and controllers.

Not all controller-pilot relationships are contentious ones. Although all airlines are officially equal and are generally handled on a first come, first served basis, some airlines are more "equal" than others. Sharp flying and a cooperative attitude gives some airlines an edge as controllers reciprocate the support they get from certain pilots. Here's a sampling of controllers' comments about airlines flying into and out of Los Angeles International.

"A lot of the Pacific Southwest pilots will volunteer to make things a little easier for you, like taking a longer downwind coming east over Santa Monica to let somebody else land; or they'll be telling you, 'We'll clear [the runway] at the first turnoff'; or they'll tell you the cloud tops without your having to ask. They'll do things like that."

"Western knows their way around pretty well, but they're bitchers. 'What are you slowing us down for?' 'Why do we have to do it that way?' 'Why can't we go now?' Grumble, grumble, grumble. If you could put up with their bitching I guess they'd be O.K."

"The TWA terminal is down toward the west end of the runway, so some of their pilots like to stay on the runway instead of turning off and having to taxi. You tell them 'First available high-speed turn-off please; traffic on short final,' and they say, 'We'll do it,' and then they stay on the runway and roll down to the far end.

"Well, when he says, 'We'll do it,' the next pilot out there on final approach hears that and figures TWA will clear, so he keeps his speed up; and, when TWA fails to clear, that pilot landing behind him has got problems."

"A lot of airline pilots see their own airplane and that's all. They don't give a damn about anybody else. They're quick to criticize if you make a mistake, but if they fuck up they expect you to overlook it. They land on the wrong runways, overshoot the final approach—come in maybe too high and then have to go around again—and then get on the P.A. system to the passengers and blame it on the controller."

"For a pilot to confirm he'll do something and then disregard it is a violation of FAA regulations, but we never call them on it. But on their next takeoff TWA will pay, because why should we work our ass off only to have TWA rolling down the runway while our guy is sweating whether TWA will be off [the runway] in time to land another plane behind him, or whether he will have to ask that other plane to go around?"

"The foreigners, you pretty much have to handle with kid gloves. New Zealand, AeroMexico, Air Korea, Japan Airlines and the ones like that, you have to keep watching to make sure they understand because maybe they're embarrassed to ask you to repeat. The Latin Americans will say 'Roger' to anything whether they understand or not—maybe because they think they do."

"I know that the captain of United's flight five, a jumbo jet nonstop to New York, isn't going to do a thing for the tower; so, when it comes to a decision whether to pump Pacific Southwest or United five, I'm gonna pump Pacific Southwest because I know the Pacific Southwest pilot isn't going to sit there on the runway after I clear him [for takeoff]."

"Texas International pilots seem to know their way around quite well —and fly like rockets. If you ever need anyone to go fast, Texas and Continental are the ones. If you let them, they'd be doin' 600 from the time they call you till they cross Lima.

"I can always count on Continental. Like, if the weather's good and you want to visual [approach] them off the airplane ahead, you could say, 'Traffic twelve o'clock, five miles is a Western jet landing two five Left; advise when you have him in sight.'

"But with Continental I'll say, 'Traffic twelve o'clock, five miles is a Western jet, he'll be landing two five Left, report him in sight and keep your speed up for the right,' and the Continental always comes right back, 'Got him in sight.'

"As soon as he hears 'Keep your speed up,' his hands are going forward with the throttles as he looks out there. Maybe he doesn't see the Western, but he knows, 'Hell, I'll see him before I hit him,' so 'We see him.' On the radar you can see his speed come right up—and it makes it a lot easier for approach to build a hole to fit somebody in behind him."

"By the time a plane's number one for departure and the pilot tells you he's ready, that's it. If he's not ready for immediate [takeoff] he should say so because we have lots of planes out there on final approach committed to land; and, if that pilot doesn't move it, we won't have anyplace to put those airplanes."

"We get accused of giving Pacific Southwest preferential treatment. It's not preferential treatment; PSA flies in and out of LAX a hundred times a day and they know we've got to run a lot of squeeze plays and that the only way to get anything done is for everybody to cooperate 100 percent. Whenever you need something, just ask PSA and they'll do it for you."

"Western captains complain a lot, 'You won't let us go when we're ready to go and there's a guy on two-mile final approach—even when he's on three-mile final you won't let us go; but, when PSA's out there for takeoff and somebody's on two-mile final, you let PSA go.'

"You have to tell them, 'Well, the thing is, we know who's going to respond and who isn't, and the guys who respond to an immediate takeoff clearance are the ones who get it. When we clear you for immediate takeoff and your takeoff isn't immediate, somebody usually has to go around.' "

"We were running parallel approaches under instrument conditions and we thought we had a Hughesair flight established on final for 24 Left— and he goes right through the final approach course and lines up with 25 Right. He wasn't talking to anybody at all, so we had to pull another jet off the approach and send him around. The Hughesair missed him by maybe less than 200 feet."

"Before a pilot lands he's often talking with his company dispatcher on the radio who's telling him what his gate assignment is, but a lot of these guys come off [the runway] and don't even tell us what gate they're going to. It's imperative for us to know, especially during a rush, because sometimes they go right past the best intersection to turn them one way or the other. Then you have to hold other planes while you have to jockey him to his gate."

"Pacific Southwest is good about giving tips to departure [control]. When it's overcast they'll always tell you how high the tops are. If the tops are 2,500, departure can launch three or four takeoffs from their satellite airports, but if the tops are 5,000 they'll have to launch one at a time because they'll be in the clouds longer."

"One of the guys was on a *fam* (familiarization) trip on Pan Am not long ago [riding in the cockpit jump seat] and the tower tells this Pan Am jumbo, 'Position and hold.' He taxis out onto the end of the runway, and a minute later the tower says, 'Clear for takeoff,' and the captain calls for the pre-takeoff checklist and he and co-pilot start going down their checklist.

"The controller who's sitting in the jump seat says, 'How come you guys do this on the runway?', and the captain says, 'Well, it's a throwback to the days when we had flying boats; you'd get lined up in the channel out there and go through your pre-takeoff check list.' So the controller says, 'Yeah, but this is the 1970s, not the '40s'."

"Western Airlines and Pan Am are notorious for being slow as hell when you clear them for immediate takeoff; but AeroMexico and Mexicana—if you clear them for immediate takeoff, they're rollin'. They'll get outta town faster for you than Pacific Southwest will."

"We have a situation with some airlines where the sky can be partially obscured and barely three miles visibility and they're coming in over Santa Monica working Stadium for a visual [approach] and you'll say, 'Traffic over Downey is a seven twenty-seven for two five Left,' and the pilot says, 'In sight,' never anything else. He never says, 'Well, maybe I'll see him in a little bit.'

"So one day I'm working one of these guys and I say, 'There's a seven twenty-seven over Hollywood Park and you're following a Fairchild over the Harbor Freeway for the right and behind him is a Continental DC-ten for the left,' and he's saying, 'In sight—in sight—in sight.' So I said, 'And there's a Clipper jumbo twelve o'clock for the right,' and he says, 'In sight,' and I said, 'Hey, I lied about that Clipper,' and he says, 'So did we!' "

"I think one reason we have so much trouble with 'Clipper' is that Pan Am's flying all over the world and a particular pilot may get into LAX very infrequently. They fly most of their lives at 39,000 feet, and the arrival here is like going into the catacombs. PSA just flies California and they're up and down all day long; they're probably better at landing and taking off than flying straight and level."

"Sometimes when the least little thing goes wrong a pilot will call the A.C. and rant and rave and jump up and down and the A.C. will manage to calm him—let him know the controller's been on the position almost two hours and that we're too short-handed for any breaks and the guy's had to eat his dinner on the position and that the instruction that was given was the only one that could be given at the time—and finally the pilots says, 'Oh, if that's the way it was, I understand.' Then he goes and writes a complant letter to the FAA Air Carrier District Office anyway.

"You have certain airlines whose pilots are repeaters; other airlines you never get a call from."

"They work twenty-five years to make captain of a 747. It's a lot of responsibility and they're good at it, and I think it kind of sticks in their craw for some twenty-nine-year-old controller to tell them where to take their 747. I think it really bothers a lot of them—sort of eats into their macho trip."

"You really have to be careful with foreign pilots; they don't know English too well and tend to hear whatever they're expecting to hear.

"The other day the Forest Service had a fire report so they called us to request we check it out with any pilots who might be in the area. I had a Mexican airliner who wasn't too far away from where the fire was supposed to be; so I called him and asked, 'Do you see anything that looks like a forest fire at about three two zero degrees from your present position and about fifteen miles away?'

"He came right back and said, 'Roger, turn left to three two zero degrees and descend to fifteen thousand feet,' and I could tell from the radar he was *doing* it. Man, I had to scramble to get him back on course awful quick!"

"Years ago when I was working at Chicago Midway, before we had radar sequencing, some of those pilots would lie your ears off. Everybody would call the tower for landing sequence, like somebody would call and say,

'Midway tower, American six twenty-one, Big Run,'—which is a reporting point about twelve miles southwest of Midway.

'American six twenty-one, Midway, roger, continue inbound; report the airport in sight.'

'American six twenty-one.'

'Midway tower, Ozark four twelve's four miles *northeast* of Big Run.'—which means he's closer to the airport than the American.

'Roger, Ozark four twelve, continue inbound, runway two two Left; report north of the airport.'

'Ozark four twelve.'

'American six twenty-one, do you have the Ozark DC-three in sight ahead?'

'Noooo,' says the American, 'but we passed him about five minutes ago.'

"So then the Ozark comes right on and says, 'We'll follow the American to the airport.'

"They'll lie like a son of a bitch about it just to be cleared to land first. They'll still lie if they think they can get away with it."

"I know United five's going to get out there on the runway and park for a while and make trouble for everybody. It's not only other controllers he's making trouble for, it's other pilots because they're lined up out there on approach and, if United five doesn't move, somebody's going to have to go around or have less than safe separation."

"Last week some of us were sittin' down in the cafeteria and this guy from the tower's there carrying on about stupid pilots—and all the time he's sitting there trying to slice his sandwich and he's cutting through his tie. Finally he says, 'Man, this is the toughest roast beef sandwich I ever saw.'"

23

Los Angeles
Center

I'm busier than shit and this Western flight comes off San Diego going to Salt Lake City and he calls me coming up on Thermal. 'Los Angeles Center, Western six with you climbing to twenty-three thousand,' and I say, 'Western six, climb and maintain three seven zero; contact center now one three three point two.' And he says, 'I can't believe it; that's the sixth frequency change I've had in twenty seconds.'

That was it, it just got to me; so I said, 'Western six, I'll tell you what; you come down here, work with radar that goes out every five minutes, radio frequencies you can't hear anything on, work rotating shifts, work overtime and make $19,000 a year; and I'll come up there, change frequencies every twenty seconds, and make $50,000 a year and be happy as hell doing it.' He didn't say another thing except, 'Going to one three three point two.'

THE LOS ANGELES Enroute Air Traffic Control Center sixty miles northeast of Los Angeles is one of twenty-one centers spread around the United States which are responsible for air traffic control in the vast areas of formerly "open" airspace between hundreds of airport terminals. From the moment a plane leaves the jurisdiction of departure control moments after takeoff, until its pilot communicates with an approach controller moments before landing, every airliner, every corporate and military jet, and every private plane on an instrument flight plan is under the air traffic jurisdiction of controllers at en route centers. A flight leaving New York for Los Angeles is worked by en route controllers in centers at New York, Cleveland, Indianapolis, Kansas City, Denver, Alberquerque, and Los Angeles who monitor the progress of planes on radar from one area to another; maintain contact with pilots; and handle flight plan modifications made necessary by potential traffic conflicts, by pilot requests, and by changing weather.

To some pilots, en route controllers monitoring their flights are welcome shepherds; to others, they are an unwelcome irritant intruding into their private and personal domain of the skies.

Los Angeles Center is a ready-made movie set. Its vast expanse of four-story-high, hundreds-of-feet-long, windowless, sand-colored brick walls is more ominous, in its own big-government way, than any Charles Addams haunted house. Its flat roof bristles with more antennas than an Ian Fleming Russian embassy. They could be plotting anything in there—anything at all. There's a high, chain-link fence and a guard house where you show your pass. Visitors—aliens—are issued red badges and must be escorted at all times. Signs warn that cameras are not allowed and security men with close-cropped hair and dark suits inquire into the contents of your briefcase. Of course there are no dark plots afoot. Whole classes of school kids visit FAA centers; your civic club probably could too, with enough notice. Aviation people are always welcome; in fact, center controllers are a bit disappointed that more airline pilots don't stop by to learn how the air traffic system works. But, at any moment, the center's radars and controllers are responsible for thousands of lives; each center has certain jobs to do in the event of war; and there have been a few threats—hence, the security measures.

If Los Angeles tower's seven-controller shift is a family, and the TRACON's fourteen men per watch are a club, Los Angeles center's hundred-controller-plus shift can best be described as two acres of very close strangers. They're not all strangers of course; many controllers there do know each other, but it's possible to work at the center for years and never know some other controller who does the same job. The sense of size, of compressed time, and vast space—and the responsibility you share, sometimes on short notice, with a controller you've never even met—all add to the sense of alienation experienced by many of the 438 controllers who work the traffic at Los Angeles center. It's just one more stress point in their daily diet of tension and anxiety and frustration. The en route center is the FAA's GM assembly line, its boiler room, its block-square insurance company office filled with faceless workers and scores of radarscopes tended by controllers who can only succeed at their jobs by really trying.

Controllers' radarscopes in the center aren't really radars. They're computer-generated, numerically-encoded displays of what the radar sees. The center's controllers work their traffic looking at twenty-two-inch, bright-green-on-black, TV tube plan view displays (PVDs). The room in which center controllers spend their working hours is banked along the walls of its 300-foot length with radar displays tilted back a few degrees from vertical. Computer keyboards and trackballs are recessed into the nine-inch-wide horizontal "desk" area in front of each radar. The center of the 300- by 185-foot room is also filled with radar displays; the room's length is bisected by two long rows of face-to-face radar positions and separated by a thick wall of electronic equipment which animates and powers each position's radar display and communications apparatus. The new, computer-fed radar display and its control console constitute a versatile combination of equipment. The controller can govern the range covered by the display he sees—from six miles to four hundred. (Two hundred miles is the normal working range in a center; fifty in a TRACON.)

The computer normally updates the controller's display with each sweep of the radar antenna, each plane's target and data block springing forward a fraction of an inch with each update. But, if he wants to keep tabs on his traffic's compliance with turns and heading changes, the controller can cause his display to show a half-bright *history* of where each plane was one, two, three, four, or five antenna-sweeps ago. He can move each plane's data block to any one of eight positions relative to the target: left, right, above, below, etc. He can also move the data block closer or farther from the target. All this is important in order to keep data blocks separate and legible when planes are flying close to each other. There's a vector line-control which can show the controller where a plane will be one, two, four, or eight minutes from any point in time—useful in quickly determining if heading changes should be issued to keep converging planes apart. The controller can also set his controls to filter out the enhanced radar targets and data blocks of all aircraft which are above or below his sector of airspace. That keeps his display from becoming cluttered with planes he's not responsible for.

The new computer-fed and digitized radar will do other things. It will show the location of precipitation and even differentiate, to some extent, between moderate precipitation and heavy precipitation—something pilots want to avoid, since heavy precipitation usually means turbulent thunderstorms. The center's data blocks are different from the TRACON's, which show only flight number, altitude, and groundspeed. Center data blocks normally display flight number, altitude, and the computer number of each plane's center. Other information—assigned climb or descent, emergency, hand-off, loss of radar contact, etc.—can also be displayed. The following data block,

NW169
390↑250
365H–36

is Northwest Orient Airlines flight 169, assigned to 39,000 feet, now climbing through 25,000. The plane's center computer num-

ber—the number under which the computer has filed the plane—
is 365, and the flight is being handed off to sector 36 within the
center's airspace.

The most highly touted feature of the new computer-fed radar
is its ability to automatically warn controllers when any two aircraft being handled by the air traffic system are in danger of
"conflict"—potential mid-air collision. The computer begins by
placing each airplane in the middle of an imaginary 2½-mile-
diameter, 2,000-foot-thick wafer of airspace. The minute the radar
sees the edges of any two planes' wafers touch—whenever they
come within 5 miles of each other laterally or within 2,000 feet of
each other vertically—their data blocks begin to blink. The warning CONFLICT ALERT also begins to blink on the controller's
radar display, listing beneath it the flight numbers of the planes
in potential conflict. The warning gives the controller time to turn
planes away from each other before they collide.

When the system is working it's very, very good; but when it's
bad—not working perfectly—it's very, very bad. The computer-
radar combination is subject to far too frequent failure, and the
CONFLICT ALERT provision has a proclivity for false alarms.
Working the system is like having to drive an expressway on bald
tires, or, as a surgeon, having to perform delicate operation after
delicate operation knowing the operating room lights could, and
probably will, go out at any time. Under conditions like that, a few
seconds in the dark can be a lifetime. And, like any system where
man is a critical component, the air traffic system is neither fool-
proof nor perfect. Things can go to hell awfully damn fast. The
responsibility is enormous. There are more than 100,000 square
miles of California, Arizona, Colorado, Nevada, and the Pacific
Ocean encompassed by Los Angeles Center's airspace. Multiply
that to include everything up to about 50,000 feet and you have
some idea of the area worked by the controllers responsible for the
thirty-three high- and low-altitude sectors into which it's all di-
vided.

The space in which controllers work is dark and subdued,
much like LAX's TRACON. The same needling and ribbing goes
on which is the essential tension-reliever in every air traffic facility,

and sometimes, when things are slow in the early hours of the morning, the humor reaches between pilots and controllers for whom recognition of each other's voice must pass for human contact.

"American ninety-five, remain on top of your present altitude; if now above your present altitude, remain above that altitude."

"Los Angeles Center, American ninety-five, we can't fly that high."

"American ninety-five, Los Angeles Center, O.K., sir, then remain above your present altitude."

"American ninety-five."

"Los Angeles Center, United one nineteen."

"United one nineteen, Los Angeles Center, go ahead sir."

"Center, United one nineteen, say your present position."

"United one nineteen, Los Angeles Center, I'm seated sir."

"Thank you very much, United one nineteen."

Controllers' on-the-job humor is about the only relief from tension they find at work; no stroll around the block or the bit of lunch-hour shopping indulged in by many office and professional workers. The ready-room at Los Angeles Center is much larger than the TRACON's, but just as blah. There's a government-issue cafeteria though, and a small patio furnished with picnic-tables where controllers can come out from their darkened radar room for lunch at noon, blinking like moles or groundhogs in the bright desert sun.

24　Sector 19

The main thing, if you're a good controller, is to stay calm and not do things drastically. Talk fast and deliver it, but if you start to lose your cool you've had it. Sometimes there will be fifteen planes yelling at me and I'll just sit back for two or three seconds, look at the whole picture, sort out everything, and make a plan. It doesn't have to be far-reaching because you'll have to change it two or three times a minute, but just enough so you can jump back in there and do it again.

SECTOR 19 is one of thirty-three oddly-shaped pieces of airspace which are controlled by Los Angeles Center. Sectors 1 through 22 are low-altitude, 23,000 feet and below; sectors 24 through 40 are high-altitude, 23,000 feet and above. There's no sector 1, 2, 16, 17, 23, 24, or 29. In all, they extend about 375 miles east of Los Angeles; 175 miles westward over the Pacific; southward to Mexico; and, to the north, almost as far as San Francisco. In square miles, Los Angeles Center's control area falls just a bit short of Texas.

Sector 19, a right-leaning, seventy- by eighty-mile parallelogram with its base touching a line which runs almost due east of Los Angeles, covers a few more square miles than the state of Connecticut. It's also the sector where more airplanes come together from more different destinations than in any other area controlled by Los Angeles Center. Sector 19 is a pressure point on the nervous system of any controller who works it. Sometimes it seems to the radar controller working "19" that every airplane in the world is aimed at him. There are three *windows* into his airspace through which most of his traffic is focused—radio navigational stations named: Hector, 130 miles northeast of LAX; Twenty-Nine Palms, 155 miles almost due east of LAX; and Blythe, 220 miles southeast.

There's another radio fix, an airway intersection just inside Sector 19's southeast corner, called Thermal.

East and south and north of Sector 19's windows, the jet airways which connect the nation's major cities begin to come together, with hundreds of gleaming jets bound for Los Angeles moving like shining droplets of water along an invisible spiderweb of radio-defined airways.

By the time they get to Hector, seven airways reaching across the United States from New York and Washington, D.C., and from Florida and Chicago and Canada have become a single, crowded line across the sky.

Jet airway 50 is aimed straight at the heart of Sector 19, via Blythe, all the way from Florida. And J 134 (another airway reaching westward from Washington, D.C.) and J 10 from Denver pierce their way into Sector 19 from Twenty-Nine Palms.

In all, thirteen airways are narrowed down to three at Hector, Twenty-Nine Palms, and Blythe. The controller working Sector 19 must somehow sort, and somehow focus all of this traffic—into a single line of perfectly spaced airliners at uniform speed, which will be handed off to the harried approach radar controller working Downey at LAX.

The Sector 19 controller has a few tools the Downey man seldom gets to use: altitude and room to vector aircraft for delay or separation. His hand-off man accepts most traffic at 24,000, and

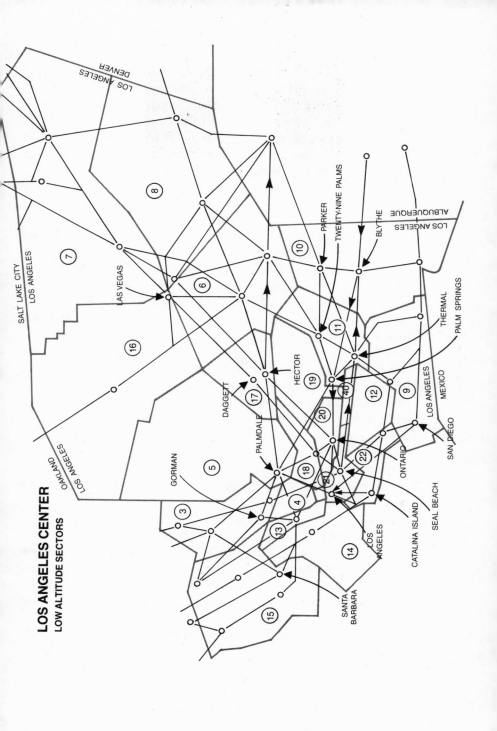

LOS ANGELES CENTER
LOW ALTITUDE SECTORS

Sector 19 hands off most of its airplanes at 15,000; so, within that range and the maneuvering limits of his airplanes, the Sector 19 controller can use altitude assignments to keep his airplanes apart. And, like TRACON approach controllers, he uses speed control. But, unlike the LAX approach controller, he's working with several converging lines of traffic—and they're moving a lot faster than they are when handed off to Downey.

6:06 PM / May 29

A Boeing 747, United 111 inbound from Chicago, is handed off to Sector 19 and makes its first call to the radar controller:

"Los Angeles, United one eleven crossing Hector." His altitude is displayed as part of his plane's data block so he doesn't report it. Many pilots, either out of habit or for safety's sake, report how high they are on their first call even though their data block is doing the job.

"United one eleven, Los Angeles, roger."

"American seventy-nine with you, slowing to three zero zero [knots] and going down to two five zero [25,000 feet]."

"American seventy-nine, roger.

"United six thirty-seven, cross Citrus intersection at, and maintain, one five thousand. Ontario altimeter two nine point eight nine."

"Cross Citrus at fifteen, United six thirty-seven."

"United one eleven, fly heading one nine zero; vector for spacing."

"One nine zero on the heading for United one eleven."

Slowly the pilot of the United 747 turns southward, away from possibly conflicting traffic he doesn't even see. Westbound, almost directly into the lowering sun, United 111 is facing almost zero forward-visibility and is forced to rely almost completely upon the Sector 19 controller to separate his airplane from scores of others also headed toward LAX.

"Los Angeles, American five, flight level two four zero (24,000 feet) at three zero zero [knots] indicated."

"American five, Los Angeles, roger."

"United eight eighty-nine, descend and maintain one seven thousand. Traffic twelve o'clock, eight miles; it's a Grumman at one six thousand."

(No response.)

"Hughesair eight eighty-nine, Los Angeles."

"Hughesair eight eighty-nine, go ahead."

"Hughesair eight eighty-nine, descend and maintain one seven thousand. Traffic one o'clock, five miles, a Grumman at one six thousand."

"Hughesair eight eighty-nine, down to maintain one seven thou'."

During the eighteen seconds which elapsed between the time the controller mis-called Hughesair 889—referring to it as United 889—and by the time he correctly called the flight, the Hughesair and the Grumman moved three miles closer to each other. There was no hazard involved because of altitude separation, but if pilots' acknowledgments were not required to "validate" an instruction, the error might have gone un-noticed.

"Los Angeles Center, Aero Commander one twenty-three Golf with you at sixteen point five [16,500]."

"Commander one twenty-three Golf, Los Angeles, radar contact."

"United one eleven, descend [and], maintain one five thousand. Ontario altimeter two nine point eight nine."

"Down to one-five thousand for United 111."

"American seventy-nine, turn left, heading one nine zero; vector for spacing."

"One nine zero for spacing, American seventy-nine."

"United six three seven, contact Los Angeles Center one three four point seven five."

"One thirty-four and three-quarters, so long, United six thirty-seven."

Now in trail with other airliners headed toward LAX, United 637 is handed off by Sector 19 to Sector 20, which will fine-tune the inbound airliners' speed and distance in the few moments remaining before they're handed off to Downey.

"American seventy-nine, descend, maintain one-five thousand. Ontario altimeter two nine point eight nine."

"Ontario altimeter two nine point eight nine"—each time the controller issues an altitude assignment he transmits the current barometric pressure at the closest ground reporting point. Planes' altimeters are really special barometers designed to display the plane's altitude above sea-level, and, since planes quickly fly from one type of weather into another, their altimeters must be frequently "updated" with correct barometric pressure settings.

Many planes carry radar altimeters which bounce electronic pulses off the ground to obtain altitude, but that's height above the *ground*—useful in making instrument landings but useless en route since cruising altitude assignments are based upon altitude above sea-level.

"TWA seven fifty-three with you out of two-six-zero for two-four-zero and we're doing three zero zero knots."

"TWA seven fifty-three, roger."

"Speedbird five ninety-nine," reports the English-accented voice of the British Airways pilot whose wide-body DC-10 departed London nearly eight hours before, "we are out of two six zero for two four zero, speed is three zero zero knots."

"Speedbird five ninety-nine, roger."

"United one eleven, turn right, heading two twenty, and intercept the ILS, runway two five Left."

"Right to two two zero for the two five Left ILS, United one eleven."

The controller has taken advantage of a space in his converging lines of inbounds and "tossed one into the glove" of the Sector 20 controller by lining the plane up with the runway prior to hand-off. Having worked the sector many times himself, he can see by looking at Sector 20's portion of his radar display that he's not setting up a problem for the Sector 20 controller—and he knows the small favor will be appreciated. He does, however, keep United 111 on his frequency until he makes the hand-off.

"Hughesair eight eighty-nine's at one seven thousand."

"Hughesair eight eighty-nine, roger."

"Where's the traffic for eight eighty-nine, now?"

"You're three miles in trail sir; he's at one five thousand."

"Eight eighty-nine."

"United one eleven, contact Los Angeles Center one three four point seven five."

"Three four point seven five, United one eleven."

Now the Sector 19 controller completes the United 111 hand-off to Sector 20, changing the plane from Sector 19 to Sector 20's radio frequency. The Sector 19 hand-off man initiated the hand-off to "20" using his trackball, and just as United 111's data block vanished from the Sector 19 radar display the controller knew the hand-off had been accepted, and issued the frequency change.

"American five, turn left, heading one nine zero; vector for spacing."

"One nine zero now for American five."

"American five, descend and maintain one four thousand, Ontar—correction, descend-maintain one five thousand. Ontario altimeter two nine point eight nine."

"American five, down to fifteen."

The controller could have said, "American five, turn left, heading one nine zero, vector for spacing, and descend to one five thousand." By issuing instructions separately the way he did, he used more air time, but reduced the chance of error.

"Center, did you call Hughesair eight eighty-nine?"

"Negative eight eighty-nine. Hughesair eight eighty-nine, descend and maintain nine thousand. Contact Ontario approach one one nine point six five."

"Down to nine and Ontario one one nine point six five for Hughesair eight eighty-nine."

When Hughesair 889 asked, "Center, did you call Hughesair?" it was probably to remind the controller that the flight was still at 17,000 and must soon begin its descent. The controller's immediate response, directing descent to 9,000 feet, suggests he may have slipped up in not starting Hughesair down a bit earlier. Pilot or controller, you try and handle these little situations diplomatically. Both sides of every conversation are being taped, by the FAA and by the airline's cockpit voice recorder aboard the plane.

"TWA seven fifty-three, descend-maintain one five thousand. Ontario altimeter two nine point eight nine."

"Descent to fifteen thousand for TWA seven fifty-three. Any turbulence reported north of San Bernadino?"

"No sir.

"TWA seven fifty-three, turn left, heading one nine zero degrees for spacing."

"Left one nine zero degrees for spacing, TWA seven fifty-three."

"American seventy-nine, say speed."

"Three hundred knots, American seventy-nine."

"Roger.

"Speedbird five ninety-nine, fly heading one nine zero; vector for spacing."

"Speedbird five ninety-nine, left to one nine zero for spacing. We're level, two four zero."

By reporting his altitude "level, two four zero" the pilot of Speedbird is asking, ever so politely, for a lower altitude as soon as possible.

"Los Angeles, United two twenty-seven at two four zero."

"Is that United two twenty-seven that called?"

"Affirmative, United two twenty-seven, level two four zero."

"Roger, two twenty-seven, radar contact."

"Los Angeles, TWA twenty-seven four zero."

"TWA twenty-seven, roger.

"American two thirty-five—correction—Western two thirty-five, fly heading one nine zero; vector for spacing.

"TWA twenty-seven, fly heading one nine zero, vector for spacing."

"A hundred and ninety on the heading, TWA twenty-seven."

"Western two thirty-five, level two-two thousand, heading one nine zero, three zero zero knots on the speed."

"Western two thirty-five, roger."

The controller called Western 235 immediately after hand-off, without waiting for the pilot to report. The pilot's inclusion of his altitude and speed in his response to the heading assignment took care of anything he might have included in his initial call to Sector 19.

"American seventy-nine, turn right, heading two two zero; intercept the ILS runway, two five Left."

"Two two zero, intercept the ILS runway, two five Left, American seventy-nine."

"American five, turn left, heading one eight zero."

"One eight zero for American five."

"American seventy-nine, contact Los Angeles Center one three four point seven five."

"Thirty-four seven point five, American seventy-nine. So long."

"Los Angeles Center, American three eighty-three, level two four zero."

"Aircraft calling center, say again."

"American three eighty-three at two four zero."

"American three eighty-three, roger."

"American two eighty-three, with you, two four zero."

"American calling center, say again."

"American two eighty-three, two four zero."

"You say American two eighty-three?"

"Roger sir, American two eighty-three, level two four zero."

"American three eighty-three?"

"American three eighty-three, roger, level two four zero."

"O.K., I got you guys sorted out now. American three eighty-three, radar contact. American two eighty-three, radar contact."

American 283 and American 383 were handed off to Sector 19 almost simultaneously, but American 283's hand-off was a few seconds premature—its data block a few seconds late appearing on the radar display. American 283, inbound from Dallas–Ft. Worth; and American 383, inbound from Knoxville, Tennessee, are both scheduled to land at Ontario International Airport at almost exactly the same time.

Time: 6:11   Elapsed time: five minutes.

During the previous five minutes the Sector 19 radar controller has never been working less than a dozen planes simultaneously. As the arrival rush builds he can expect to be working fifteen, twenty, perhaps twenty-two or twenty-three airplanes at the same time. He will continue to work the position another fifty-five minutes before being relieved.

And, when the equipment is working perfectly, he loves it.

25

Disaster
for Dessert

Where you really earn your money as an air traffic con-
troller is when somebody fucks up and all of a sudden,
just like that, you gotta do something and it's got to be
in the next second and it's got to be right—or you're
gonna have a deal.

SECTOR 19 wasn't where it happened, but it
could have been. Traffic had been light, certainly no more than
moderate, when the hand-off controller working the Wayne (high
altitude) sector at Cleveland Center went to lunch shortly before
7:00 P.M. When the hand-off controller signed off the position, the
radar and hand-off positions were combined. A third member of
the sector team, called the "manual" controller, continued his
duties updating flight progress strips and coordinating with adjacent sectors and other facilities. Ten aircraft, fewer than he often
handled, were being worked by the radar controller when he
accepted American 182, a DC-10 jumbo jet en route to Newark,
from Chicago Center.

Making his first contact with the radar controller as he entered
the Wayne sector's airspace, the pilot reported:

"Cleveland Center, American one eighty-two heavy [jumbo jet] with you out of flight level two eight zero [28,000 feet] for three seven zero [37,000 feet]."

The radar controller verified American 182's position and compared the plane's data block on his radar display with its flight progress strip. According to the data block, American 182 was on course along jet airway 584, 100 miles west of the Carleton, Michigan, VOR climbing out of 26,200 feet toward its assigned altitude of 37,000 feet. The discrepancy between American 182's reported altitude of 28,000 feet and the data block's indication of 26,200 feet didn't unduly concern the controller, since he knew that radar data was updated only once every twelve seconds, the time it took the radar's antenna to make a complete sweep of its coverage area. There were no antenna sweeps visible on the display; targets just sprung forward and data blocks were updated five times a minute. Within another thirty seconds the controller determined that American 182 was climbing at the rate of about 1,000 feet a minute at a groundspeed of 540 mph.

Looking at his radar display, the controller noted that American 182, eastbound toward the Carleton VOR on J-584, might later come into conflict with TWA 37, another jumbo jet, westbound at 37,000 feet along the same airway. During its climb to 37,000 feet, American 182 would pass through TWA 37's assigned altitude. There would be time, the controller was sure, to issue a heading change for American 182 if any possibility of the planes coming too close to each other appeared likely.

Soon after he sized up the situation, the controller became absorbed in attempting to enter a flight plan change for a Learjet into the Center computer, which kept refusing to accept the data. Learning from the manual controller that he had no flight strip on the Learjet, the radar controller sent him to the sector originally included in the Learjet's flight plan. He found the flight strip there and brought it back to the Wayne sector.

At 7:21, American 182 was forty-six miles west of TWA 37, climbing through 33,000 feet. The two jumbo jets were headed directly toward each other along the same airway at a combined speed of nearly 1,000 mph. At their current closure rate of fifteen miles every sixty seconds, they would meet head-on in a devastating mid-air collision in less than three minutes.

At 7:22, the radar controller monitoring American 182 and TWA 37, plus eight or nine other aircraft on the display, was relieved by the controller who had just returned from lunch.

In briefing his relief, the controller going off duty failed to point out the now acute potential conflict between the two jumbo jets.

At 7:22:05, five seconds after he sat down at the radar display, the controller became involved in a conversation with several aircraft, responding to a request for information about the height of the top of the overcast:

7:22:05—Cleveland Center, United six eighty, any idea of the tops?"

7:22:08—Well, they were at three five zero earlier, just a minute, let me check.

7:22:13—*TWA thirty-seven, Cleveland Center, what are the tops?"*

7:22:17—They are higher than we are; it's hard to say. You can see through it; I'd say they must be at least three seven zero.

7:22:25—*O.K., TWA thirty-seven, thank you.*

7:22:29—*United six eighty, did you copy?*

7:22:31—Yes, thank you.

At 7:22:38, another aircraft, American 26, reported that it was just skimming the cloud tops.

7:22:42—*O.K., American twenty-six, thank you.*

7:22:43—*United six eighty, that aircraft is at three seven zero.*

At 7:22:45, as he was scanning the radar after completing his conversation with United 680, the controller suddenly noticed—

1. that American 182's data block showed it was at 34,500 feet climbing to its assigned altitude of 37,000;

2. that TWA 37's data block showed the flight level at 35,000 feet;

3. that the two planes were twelve o'clock to each other and only three or four miles apart.

In stark disbelief, hoping that American 182's actual altitude was higher than the figure shown by the data block, the controller called the flight.

7:22:52—*American one eighty-two, Cleveland, what is your altitude?*

7:22:55—American one eighty-two, passing through three four point seven at this time, and we can see the stars above us, but we're still in the area of the clouds.

7:23:03—*American one eighty-two, descend immediately to three three zero!*

7:23:06—Descending to three three zero at this time.

7:23:11—*TWA thirty-seven, traffic twelve o'clock and a mile descending out of three four point five.*

When the controller issued its emergency descent, American 182 was flying on instruments in and out of the clouds. At the moment the aircraft started an immediate descent, the captain, first officer, and flight engineer sighted the lights of TWA 37 in their twelve o'clock position. As he shouted, "There he is!", the captain applied strong forward pressure on the control wheel to avoid the other plane. He later estimated that the distance between the two aircraft as they passed was no more than 100 feet.

On his radar display, the controller watched the targets for American 182 and TWA 37 merge and—twelve seconds later—separate.

The seatbelt sign had been on throughout the entire length of American 182's forty-five-minute flight from Chicago, but meals were being served when the captain suddenly pushed the control wheel forward to avoid TWA 37. Stewardesses, heavy service carts, food, trays, and four passengers who didn't have their seatbelts fastened were thrown against the roof of the cabin by the negative "G" forces as the captain dove the plane toward the ground. During the transition from negative to positive gravity conditions as American 182 leveled out at 33,000 feet, the service carts, ten stewardesses, and four passengers who were momentarily pinned against the overhead, came down heavily, striking the floor, cabin seats, and other passengers. Fourteen passengers and all ten stewardesses were injured, several seriously. No one was killed.

Although one of the pilots aboard TWA 37 thought he had briefly seen the lights of another plane, none of the TWA crew were aware of the near mid-air until they landed in Los Angeles.

After leveling out at 33,000 feet, the captain of American 182 requested immediate clearance for descent to the nearest airport which could take the jumbo jet. Upon landing in Detroit the plane's injured passengers were taken to hospitals. There were no injuries in the cockpit, nor was there any structural damage to the plane. There were 13 crewmembers and 192 passengers aboard American 182, and 11 crewmembers and 103 passengers aboard TWA 37. It would have been the worst mid-air collision in aviation history.

Unlike the 1956-collision between United 718 and TWA 2 which resulted, more than anything else, from lack of adequate radar and communications equipment, the controllers working American 182 and TWA 37 had everything which controllers of a few years ago could wish for. Their radar resolved aircraft positions so accurately that separation standards along airways were five miles, instead of the old ten minutes flying time. Radar targets were associated with data blocks which told each plane's number, altitude, and groundspeed. Communications were instant, long-range, free of weather interference, and reliable. Though still far from perfect, air traffic control equipment had been so vastly improved that human beings were now the weakest link. A 1975-study of air traffic errors resulting in less than the required aircraft separation indicated that 96 percent, resulting in twenty-one near mid-air collisions, were human errors.

Soon after the 1975 near mid-air collision between the two jumbo jets over Carleton, Michigan, the FAA's air traffic computers were programmed to blink the targets and data blocks of planes on a controller's radar display *before* their courses produced an acute danger of mid-air collision. But controllers say the new system, called **CONFLICT ALERT** is guilty of many false alarms.

26   Frank Galla

*People think controllers are like in "Airport": mass con-
fusion, people dropping over from ulcers. I think if that
were true there wouldn't be any air traffic controllers.
But everybody has their moment, like being a policeman.
Sooner or later in air traffic control the time comes, just
like with a cop—whether to shoot or not—and you'd
better be right.*

HIGH ABOVE the Arizona desert United Air-
lines flight 11, nonstop from Newark to Los Angeles, moves across
the deep blue of the late afternoon sky. Inside the giant, swept-
wing airliner, 38,000 feet above the desert floor, more than 150
passengers doze, knit, review sales presentations, total up expense
accounts, and fantasize of licit and illicit love. On the plane's flight
deck, the captain and first officer arrange their Los Angeles charts
close at hand and begin to review the litany of in-range and
pre-descent checklists which they will soon recite together as part
of the studied ritual of bringing their 335,000-pound DC-8 safely
to the ground. In a few moments, halfway between Prescott, Arizona, and Grommet, site of the closest radio navigational station

ahead, air traffic responsibility for their flight will be handed off by the Albuquerque Center to Los Angeles.

Two hundred and fifty miles to the west of United 11, twenty-nine-year-old Los Angeles Center controller Frank Galla is nearing the end of his fourth hour on shift. For the last fifteen minutes of that time he has been sitting at the elbow of the radar controller whose position he will soon be working. Together they watch the silent blips and data blocks which sometimes move in seeming random fashion—like water spiders on the still, green surface of a summer pond. The area of Frank Galla's responsibility is one of thirty-three fragments which form the airspace controlled by Los Angeles Center. With practiced proficiency, Galla's mind is becoming part of the man-machine-computer complex which, during his eight-hour shift, will thread hundreds of airplanes onto the instrument landing system of Los Angeles International Airport. When both men are sure he "has the picture," the lightweight earphones and boom-microphone which Galla wears will become one terminus of an electronic nervous system which no one yet fully understands, and he will assume air traffic responsibility for the scores of airliners and other planes which will enter and leave his airspace. Soon, Galla will slip into the seat in front of the radar display, and, with only the change of his voice for that of the controller he relieves, he will be accountable for more lives than he can comfortably comprehend.

The weather is good, for Los Angeles: clear sky with seven miles visibility in what the continuous aviation weather broadcast refers to as "smoke and haze." But, for United 11 and every other aircraft headed into the late afternoon sun, it is considerably less than that.

Aboard United 11, just as the plane passes over the twelve-mile-long lake formed by a dam across the Santa Maria River, Albuquerque Center's hand-off to Los Angeles takes place as both pilots expected.

"United eleven, contact Los Angeles Center now, one three three point five five."

"Los Angeles on one three three point five five, United eleven, so long."

Changing to the new frequency, the pilot of United 11 makes his initial contact with Los Angeles Center.

"Los Angeles Center, United eleven with you, flight level three nine zero."

"United eleven, Los Angeles, radar contact."

The exchange between United 11 and the sector east of his isn't heard by Frank Galla, but he knows from previous experience that his hand-off man will soon be hearing from the other sector, and the target and blinking data block which represent United 11 will soon be appearing at the edge of his radar display.

As United 11's data block begins blinking at the edge of Galla's sector, his hand-off man accepts the flight and its data block remains a bright, steady, green moving toward the point upon which a score of other planes in Galla's sector are also converging.

As soon as Sector 19 accepts the hand-off, the Sector 37 controller, whose airspace the airliner is now leaving, instructs United 11 to contact Sector 19.

"United eleven, contact Los Angeles Center now, one two six point three five."

"Goin' to one two six point three five, United eleven. So long."

"United eleven with you, two four zero," reports the pilot, making his first radio contact with Frank Galla.

On Frank Galla's radar display, the dozen or so planes he was working before United 11's arrival, and the half dozen additional flights which have simultaneously flooded into his sector, have become almost too much. Suddenly, Galla's airspace has become incredibly small, just the way all that paper which a bank teller is counting suddenly turns into *money.* Everybody is converging on United 11: inanimate airliners a moment ago, they are now a pack of sharks converging on an unsuspecting victim, United 11. United 11 and the planes surrounding it are now almost all at fifteen thousand and there is no room to turn anyone without invading someone else's airspace or placing one plane on collision course with another.

"Los Angeles, Continental six zero five with you, two four zero."

"Continental six zero five, Los Angeles, roger, radar contact."

Pilots call and Galla answers, wishing only to be left alone to figure out the mounting problem presented by the sharks converging on unsuspecting United 11 in the center of his radar. In seconds the warning on his display will begin flashing "CONFLICT ALERT—UA 11/AA 427; or UA 11/UA 799"; or both of the above.

In Sector 19's airspace, the pilot and first officer of United 11 see only the glowing golden haze created by a glaring sun burning at them through the smog and pollution of the Los Angeles basin straight ahead. It would be impossible to see the Goodyear blimp if it were hanging right in front of them.

Aware that he is fast approaching the point at which he must be turned inbound toward Los Angeles, and concerned about the now unaccounted for silence on the frequency, the pilot of United 11 calls Los Angeles Center:

"Los Angeles, United eleven."

(Silence)

"Los Angeles, United eleven."

At his radar, Frank Galla suddenly turns to the radar controller working the position next to his:

"Cliff, I've lost it! I don't know what to do! I don't know what to do!"

"At the time," he says, "I was scared half to death. Cliff was new and just signed off on his sector and didn't know what to do either. I had to do something immediately. All of a sudden I said, 'Hey, wait a minute, if I just move *United 11,* everything else will fall into place. With God only knows how much effort to keep my voice sounding calm and steady, I called the United:

'United eleven, right turn zero six zero degrees, vector for spacing.' And that United pilot came right back:

'Right to zero six zero United eleven; level one five zero.'

"God, he must have suspected something because that's a hell of an unusual call, but he never said a word. Two planes passed behind him—and it worked! All I had to do was vector that one airplane, like pulling a certain place on a tangled knot, and the tangle all unravels."

Galla's next call to United 11 brought the airliner almost through a complete circle, headed toward LAX and safely behind the pack of sharks which had once again become airplanes.

Aboard United 11 the flight's lead stewardess was speaking into the plane's public address system: "Ladies and gentlemen, we are now approaching the Los Angeles landing area and the captain asks that you place your seat backs in the upright position and fold your seat trays into the receptacle in front of you. The weather in Los Angeles is clear and the temperature is 82 degrees. Thank you for flying United."

For the passengers, another routine, predictable, safe flight.

"You work traffic," Galla explains, "and the first five of six years it's really neat. It's different. It's exciting—challenging. It taxes your mental and even physical skills. How fast can you press the keyboard to talk to the computer and flip things when it's really important to do it right the first time? It's beautiful; it's just lovely going to work, especially if the equipment's working that day. There are five or six times in my career when I've done a brilliant job, figured out things nobody could figure out; suddenly I just saw it. I knew what had to be done and I did it. It's so fantastic when you have a lot of airplanes and, without ever getting upset, or nervous, or yelling and screaming, you can just take those guys, just effortlessly, and do your thing. Those times are still so vivid. I can remember the airplanes; I can even remember the flight numbers!

"I got into air traffic control when I went into the Air Force out of high school. I had a choice of combat photographer, motion picture projectionist, or air traffic controller. I said I'd take air traffic control school. I thought air traffic controllers were those guys with flashlights out on the ramp that show the pilots where to park. I took the test for air traffic controller and passed it and later they gave me a little booklet that told me what it was all about. I fell in love with it, especially when they told me that if I flunked I'd be a cook or air policeman; so I graduated at the top of my class. It was the first job in my life I ever loved.

"Working in the tower, and in approach control, is entirely different from center work. I was a good tower controller and I was a hell of a good approach controller. I could sit down there at the radar and just fly. I loved it. It was neat. I could do it right and I could do it fast.

"When I first came here to the center I almost washed out on a slow sector. It was a molasses nightmare. I couldn't get used to the idea of long range when they put me on an oceanic sector, because there you have to plan half an hour in advance. You have 300 miles of airspace and it's only half radar and you have so many procedures and so many military outfits working out there. And working super long-range, everything is so subtle. Nothing comes right up and grabs you in the ass. In approach control you've got this guy here, and that guy there, and another guy over there; he's at four thousand; he's at five thousand. But on a big sector like the oceanic you have so many, and they seem so far apart, that it looks like you've got time to go to lunch, and then all of a sudden, zap, there two of 'em are, converging and you thought they'd never be less than a hundred miles apart.

"Here at the center we have so many sectors that you have to watch out that some guy working on the other side of the room, who maybe you've never met in your life, doesn't fuck you. He can hand a guy at another sector a near mid-air without him knowing he's got it until he's screwed. It doesn't help either that the equipment doesn't work. One day I was working Sector 40 and I had about eight aircraft all converging on Thermal at the same time. I was vectoring and just finessing them in there—and the radar goes blank. So I think, 'Oh shit!' and I get over in front of the flight strips and call every airplane, 'What's your altitude?—What's your altitude?—What's your altitude?—What's your altitude?', knowing that if I couldn't see them I'd have to get them to different altitudes real fast.

"The radar didn't come back until two or three minutes later. I didn't know whether I'd had a deal or not.

"I told my supervisor. 'God damn it! You expect me to work with this thing?', so he looks over and says, 'Well, you don't have any airplanes,' and I said, 'Well, you should have been here three minutes go.' He says, 'Well, hang in there.'

"So about half an hour later the same thing happens again. I had six or seven airplanes all converging on Thermal and the radar goes blank. So I got pissed; I said, 'Look, I'm not going to work that RDP (radar data processed) display any more. I'm going to control my airplanes with the back-up broadband radar.'

"He said, 'You can't stay on broadband with everybody else on RDP.' I said, 'Bullshit. It's unsafe and I'm not going to work it.'

"He said if I didn't work the RDP he was going to pull me off the sector and send me to training for two weeks. So I worked the RPD and I was afraid it was going to go out again any minute.

"Sometimes it gets really bad. You'll have about ten airplanes and the radar's going out and the frequencies don't work—I can't hear anybody and nobody can hear me—and the pilots won't cooperate. Everything just turns to shit. I've become very nervous. I bite my nails. I have nightmares. I'm over the hill as far as the center's concerned. But I'm stuck. You can't get transferred out of here. I feel like I'd really be happy in the FAA if I could just get down below in the LA basin to a small approach control or something like that; anywhere else but here. If you threaten to quit they just say, 'Fine, quit,' because they figure if they let you get away with something like that, then everybody's going to be doing it and this place would be empty overnight.

"I don't have to prove myself anymore. I've done that thousands and thousands of times. I know I'm good in a clutch, but I don't dig it any more because my nerves can't take it. If I had my choice, I'd pick music. I'd join a rock band. I don't know that I'd do it forever, but, you know, you can just get on that bus and go. I've got to get out soon; got to go. I have too many dreams. One recurring nightmare I have is where I have a deal. I've got twenty-five airplanes—I'm just loaded—and they're all coming together and my radios don't work and the radar goes off and comes back on. I can't get help from anybody. The guy working next to me won't help me; he just doesn't care. I call the assistant chief's desk and they just say, 'You'll work it out some way.' I call other facilities to try to get them to talk to the airplanes and they tell me, 'Oh, we're busy'; they just don't care either. And all the time these planes are coming together, closer and closer. There's going to be a deal—somebody's going to hit! And then the radios come back, and if I talk as fast as I can talk, I might be able to get out of it—but I can't say anything; my voice just goes, 'Uh-uh-uh-uh,' in slow motion, but I can't say anything. And just as they're all about to come together—I wake up.

"Actually, that dream isn't too far from a near deal I had a couple of years ago when I was working approach control. This MEDEVAC flight I was working departed a military base full of patients and I was watching him pretty close, just because I didn't have a lot of other traffic at the moment, when I saw this other target come up at the edge of my scope. I checked my flight strips and I didn't have anything on him, so I called the MEDEVAC and gave him the traffic and he said he didn't see him. I called the center and they said Japan Airlines was coming over. Japan Airlines must have forgotten to call me, and center didn't have him on their frequency either. The JAL flight was cleared over the VOR at 9,000, and the MEDEVAC was headed for the VOR at 9,000, so I jumped off the phone and gave the MEDEVAC, '*Immediate* right turn!' and he said, 'I can't, I have patients on board,' and I said, 'Make *immediate* right turn! Traffic twelve o'clock, opposite direction!' Those two targets merged.

"God, I was so sick! I had a feeling I've never felt before and I felt that way until those two targets separated. They never saw each other. I got Japan landed and I got off the position. I was so sick. I was shaking for four or five hours after that."

27 Carole Raymond

The thing that might seem great to a lot of controllers —to have their wife really understand their job and know what they mean when they say 'flight plan route'—doesn't work out that well. When you're both controllers one of you comes home looking for sympathy and the other just as often says, 'Well, I think you should have done it differently,' or 'That's no big thing, what are you complaining for?' I've talked to my mother who has no idea what parallel approaches are and she's said, 'Oh, honey, that's too, too bad!' That's *what I needed.*

CAROLE RAYMOND is a Los Angeles Center controller—married to a Los Angeles Center Controller—and it isn't working out. She has had to fight hostility toward women; as a couple, she and her husband have had to fight FAA bureaucracy; and, as individuals, she and the man she's married to have had to contend with the pressures of competing for the same promotion and with the reluctance of the FAA to offer advancement to either if it meant that the other could not obtain an assignment in the same location.

215

As with the legions of executives who have made their work the center of their lives, Carole admits that her career is more important to her than almost anything else. Like many male controllers, she entered air traffic control in the service. That was easy. The second time, returning to air traffic control with five young children after a broken marriage, was a triumph.

"When I was in high school," she says, "I wanted to be a journalist, but my parents didn't have any money to send me to college; so I knew I'd have to go to work. Then one day, just before graduation, a Navy recruiter came to school and he talked about a lot of different jobs and handed out booklets. I looked at the booklet on air traffic control and decided that's what I'd do. I went home and told my folks I was going to join the Navy and be an air traffic controller. My father said, 'Over my dead body!' and my mother said, 'I think that's great!' I went through the Olathe, Kansas, air controller school and when I got out was sent to Alameda Naval Air Station in California. I finally married a guy in crash salvage and right away he got sent to Hawaii. My enlistment was up just about then; so I got out of the Navy and joined him. We were in Hawaii until 1967, when we were transferred to Alameda. "I missed air traffic control all along, but my marriage felt very strong and comfortable—the feeling you get when he brings home the money and you know you're going to have hamburgers and that you're going to get a babysitter and go out on Saturday night. We had five kids then; three were ours and two by his first marriage.

"Then one day he just walked in and said, 'Here are the house keys. I'm in love with someone else and I'm leaving you to marry her.'

"I went down to San Diego to live with my mother and father and my aunt. I didn't work; I just stayed home with the children. I didn't resent the children, but I felt very sorry for me; I was wallowing in a state of self-pity: 'I can't go to work; I can't leave the kids; I can't get away from the house; I have to stay here. How can I live like this?' I would be out in the yard and I'd look up and see a jet go by and I'd think, 'Wouldn't it be neat to be in a tower again, having the jets come in and be saying, 'clear to land' and 'hold short,' and then one of the kids would start crying or something and I'd turn and go back in the house.

"Finally an old controller I knew in the Navy said, 'Why don't you get in the FAA?' and I said, 'I can't; for seven years I've been changing diapers and fixing formula,' and he said, 'No, you can do it; you were a good controller.' I thought I owed it to those who were helping me to at least make the effort; so I took the FAA exam and passed it and then passed the physical and the psychological and it just seemed to be snowballing. I was accepted as a GS-8 and my parents took care of the kids for six weeks while I went through the FAA Academy in Oklahoma City. While I was there I was beginning to realize, 'I can make something for *me.*' I was catching on, getting rid of the feeling-sorry-for-myself thing. When I graduated from the FAA Academy I was assigned to Los Angeles Center from the very beginning. I had asked for every tower in the Los Angeles basin and they sent me to the center. I didn't even know what a center did.

"I made it through training at the center, got my GS-9, and met Jim, my present husband, all in a very short time. Meeting Jim was neat because he was a widower with two children of his own and wasn't turned off by my kids. I was the fledgling and he was the experienced controller and he'd practice with me in the evening, working out problems and playing the parts of the pilots while I played the controller. We got married several months later with all seven kids and two sets of parents all there. We started in a three-bedroom house, which is pretty small when you've got all those kids and a live-in housekeeper. A couple of months after we were married the FAA said, 'Listen, this is nepotism; you both can't work in this facility.' We pointed out that there was no way Jim could influence my career or that I could influence his. I was not in his area and I had never worked or even trained under him. We were told that didn't make any difference and that one of us would have to leave. We said that Jim would take someplace else and I would remain at the center in Palmdale so we wouldn't have to move all the kids.

"You tell them what you want and the FAA tells you what you'll get. They said Jim was a highly-qualified controller and valuable and that I was new and not valuable. So they sent me to Edwards Air Force Base thirty-five miles northeast of here. The FAA handles air traffic control at Edwards. There were no women in the facility and, as the first woman, I was unwelcome there. The assistant chief, who was in charge of training, sent me a letter stating that I would not be allowed to use the controllers' bathroom until I completed training. So I had to go out the top story of the building, down two flights of stairs, through a keyed door, and across a big hangar to where there was a bathroom for the secretary.

"Finally, Jim found another controller-couple working radar and flight data at Oakland, California, and he contacted someone at the FAA regional office who pulled strings and got me back to the center. After we were back together we arranged to work the same hours, but I don't think it was really good. You sleep together, you get up together, you drive to work together, you work together—even if you're in different sectors you make hand-offs —then you drive home together and you're together all evening. Jim can come home after a really bad day and sit down and blast off about Sector 31 and the deal they handed him, and tell me they slipped him two on parallel, and I know exactly what he's talking about. But, when he's feeling all this pain, I'm feeling pain too because maybe somebody's slipped me a deal. There just isn't enough room in either of us for the sympathy the other wants. When you're doing the same job you understand the verbiage, but sometimes what I want is just a nobody who can be sympathetic. Maybe I was right or maybe I was wrong, but what I need is sympathy and not a critique. And Jim doesn't need a critique either.

"Jim has been a controller seventeen years, and he's a GS-13. I've been a controller just eight and I'm a GS-13, temporarily assigned as an [air traffic] area officer, and I'm getting GS-14 pay. We know that if I stay on this job, and he makes supervisor, the FAA will say that's nepotism and it will be. Jim needs to make supervisor; he's getting a lot of jazz about the old lady being a GS-14. I know he wants to be a GS-14 team supervisor and I want to be a GS-14. I'm good at the type of work I'm doing now, which is planning procedures and working with the military on mission planning. I've been endorsed by the management here for a GS-14 job in Washington, but there's no guarantee Jim would be able to get an assignment there. He's been interviewed for GS-14 supervisor jobs other places, but they always ask him, 'You mean you'd give up [your wife's] $25,000 a year for a $2,000 raise to come here?', and then they take somebody else because they think he wouldn't be happy. So now we're in competition for the same promotion here at the center—and if either of us gets it, then it's nepotism.

"I don't know that I'm too eager to go back to a line job because of the attitude a lot of controllers have toward women. You have to be better than a man doing the same job. I have worked beside, and have been written up for commendation by, men; but there's still that same 'macho,' 'I'm letting you play this game and you'd better be good because I'm letting you play the role.' They'll tell you, 'You're really good; I'm proud of you,' as though they are allowing you to be good. They'll tell you, 'Thanks for all the help; you really were right in there doing a super job and thanks for all the help,' but they'll never tell you, 'Carole, you did it better than I could have done it.' Jim is the only controller I've never gotten that patronizing feeling from. Jim has always been very supportive and never made me feel I was less of a person because I'm a woman on the job. But still, we sometimes get into discussions about who's working the most traffic and who's the best controller.

"Jim and I separated for a while several months ago. It was terrible. We worked the same shift and when I came to work I would try to avoid seeing him. But if he wasn't there I would notice it and I'd look at the schedule to see if he'd called in sick or something. We'd end up on coffee break at the same time, or in the cafeteria line pretending we didn't see each other. After work at night I'd stop off and have a drink at a bar with people we'd both gone there with before, only now we were going to different bars. We're back together now, but it's not comfortable. It's not a strong, 'hang in there' kind of marriage.

"I wouldn't change being an air traffic controller. I wouldn't change being a mother. But I don't know, I think I'd change being married."

28 Inside the Pressure Cooker

*If my wife doesn't have dinner ready when I get home,
I'm going to kick the hell out of her; if she does, I won't
eat a bite!*

ITWOULD be natural to wonder if the pressures
and stresses which controllers say affect their health and family
life are real, or whether they are merely the whining complaints
of 16,000 spoiled prima donnas. By every objective measure, air
traffic control at busy airports and high-density sectors at en route
centers is one of the most stressful and demanding occupations in
the United States. Controllers' on-the-job anxiety levels and vital
signs closely match those of astronauts about to be launched into
space. In describing the stress-producing demands of air traffic
control, Dr. Sebastian Dangerfield, a clinical psychologist who has
studied controller stress in both Great Britain and the United
States, reports that—The following:

1. air traffic controllers are captives of a system and have no means of
stemming the sometimes overwhelming tide of airplanes which they are
responsible for;

2. although they can sometimes work under this pressure at high levels of efficiency, they do it at a price which includes chronic anxiety, sleeplessnes, nightmares, ulcers, and impotence;

3. they must adapt to extraneous noise—buzzers, alarms, and other controllers' radio conversations which are continuously taking place around them—from which they must filter possibly critical information, something they do only at considerable psychological expense;

4. they must continuously exercise a high degree of accuracy and use extremely precise speech, knowing that the slightest slip of the tongue can cost hundreds of lives;

5. they suffer almost constant anxiety about the consequences of committing an error which may result in a mid-air collision;

6. they are subject to a short-cycle rotating schedule which disrupts family life, eliminates any possibility of normal eating and sleep patterns, and often doesn't even allow eight hours rest between shifts; and

7. unless the controller's marriage is an unusually strong one, his work-related stress can often magnify otherwise managable problems, resulting in additional stress and possible divorce—specifically, the reduced sexual capacity which often results from short-cycle shift work must be understood and accepted by the wife if the marriage is to remain intact.

An Atlanta psychiatrist, Dr. Merton Berger, who for ten years served the Federal Aviation Administration as a psychiatric consultant, examined hundreds of air traffic controllers to determine whether they were mentally and emotionally fit to safely continue in their jobs. Dr. Berger reports that

Instances of mechanical breakdown of radio and radar represent so much stress that there have been innumerable instances when an air traffic controller has collapsed at his console. This acute decomposition is less frequent however than the insidious form which occurs over months and sometimes years.

In this latter condition we sometimes see emotional and mental depression which becomes so intense that the air traffic controller begins to feel that the only way out is suicide. His sleeping patterns become so disturbed that it not only takes hours to fall asleep, but there is fitful sleep with frequent awakening during the night. The controller begins to have terrifying nightmares which become recurrent and more intense as time goes by. More often than not, the nightmare has to do with one type of incident which is the dread of all air traffic controllers, the mid-air collision.

Appetite disturbances often develop which lead to weight loss, and I have treated air traffic controllers who vomit involuntarily as they approach the control tower or traffic center.

The clinical picture presented by the air traffic controller is one of severe neurosis with one or all of the following components: anxiety, depression, and phobia.

Heart attacks have occurred while air traffic controllers have been on duty and there have been too many instances where the air traffic controller has been carried by ambulance directly from his job to the hospital for emergency treatment. From a medical point of view, the air traffic controller shows a syndrome almost identical to that found by military surgeons among front-line troops engaged in heavy fighting.

Unfortunately, the Federal Aviation Administration has not been willing to acknowledge the fact that controlling air traffic is a stressful job.

Dr. Robert Henshaw, a Los Angeles psychiatrist who treats air traffic controllers says, "Controllers I see have an overriding fear that, if they are 'working' planes involved in a mid-air collision, the FAA will try to protect itself by 'making' them responsible for it. PATCO, the air traffic controllers' union, has cautioned members against discussing any accident in which they may be involved with FAA management, unless a PATCO representative is present." In commenting on the difficulties encountered in dealing with the FAA concerning medical disability for a Los Angeles controller, Dr. Henshaw says,

It's almost as though the FAA was trying to throw obstacles in the man's way, or torture the guy with broken promises. They would send him a letter telling him that action would be taken within thirty days, and then sixty days would go by and there would be no action. When I attempted to follow up, nobody in management would seem to know what was happening. You always hear that if you're a government employee with a problem you shouldn't go to your Congressman in these cases, but, hell, I don't know what recourse is left to the guy. He was getting to the point where he was bankrupt. He had been living off savings for months with no income. The controllers' union had to send out a call for ten-dollar contributions to set up a fund he could draw on for food and rent. Finally, the FAA appointed another psychiatrist who was very quick to label the controller's breakdown a consequence of family problems. It apparently never occured to him that it could possibly be the other way around. Hell, the FAA's own psychologist said the controller's problem was strictly work-related.

The thing that gets me about controller patients I see is how many of them have indigestion, trouble sleeping, ulcers, asthma, and other illnesses which are directly related to stress and which they accept as conditions of living. But, when they stop controlling traffic, they have an almost magical remission of these symptoms. Sometimes it's hard for them to get adjusted to it. A fellow may have been eating Gelusil antacid like it was going out of style—every day several times a day—and he will go down to nothing at all. He won't have one antacid after he's gone off air traffic control duty.

The FAA says that these fellows are just trying to get a disability retirement; but I couldn't tell you how many controllers come here hoping to stay on the job, asking me not to tell the FAA.

As I reached forward from my chair in Dr. Henshaw's office and prepared to turn off my tape recorder, he held up his palm, motioning for me to wait. "There is one more thing I must say," he told me, "the two-day rotating shift schedule which the FAA subjects these people to is horrible. If I sat up nights I couldn't think of a more diabolical way to torture people. It's almost sadistic. It's so management-oriented; it has no consideration at all for people, they're just 'things.' The two-day rotating shift system looks orderly, so management uses it, but it disrupts peoples' lives completely. It creates added stress."

Dr. Henshaw's experiences treating Los Angeles air traffic controllers are echoed by Chicago psychiatrist E. Elliot Benezra, who has worked with more than seventy air traffic controllers since 1970, and who, at this writing, has more than a dozen air traffic controllers in therapy.

Dr. Benezra finds that his air traffic controller patients suffer from loss of appetite, irritability, impotence, ulcers, high blood pressure, and sever anxiety aggravated by fear of mid-air collisions. He reports that most controllers he sees would rather continue working in air traffic than change to some other career, but that they too often put off seeking help in the hope that somehow they'll be able to work through their difficulties on their own. "But by the time I see them," he says, "it's often too late. Their health and ability to handle traffic have deteriorated, their marriages have crumbled, and they are often in a state of severe depression."

In nearly every case where psychiatrists' concern about controllers has come to public attention, their opinions have been labeled by the FAA as "unscientific" or "highly subjective." One FAA official speaking to the press lumped all controllers' therapists together, saying their expressions of concern were, "self-serving statements by physicians bent upon building up a practice of individuals [who are] paying them to deliver a specific product: certification which will allow them to obtain medical retirement."

At least a part of psychiatrists' concern about controller-stress is borne out by an investigation conducted by two medical researchers, Dr. Sidney Cobb, of the Notre Dame Medical Research Center, and Dr. Robert Rose, of the Boston Medical School.

In a review of FAA medical examination records of 4,325 air traffic controllers and 8,435 commercial pilots, Drs. Cobb and Rose found that peptic ulcer, a frequent result of continued stress, was twice as prevalent among air traffic controllers as among commercial pilots.

High blood pressure, another medically recognized indicator of stress, was found to be twice as prevalent among controllers in the thirty to thirty-four age bracket as among second class airmen of the same age; and three times as prevalent among controllers of that age group working in high density air traffic facilities as among controllers assigned to low density facilities. High blood pressure was *ten* times more common among controllers in the thirty-five to thirty-nine age bracket than among second class airmen of the same age.

The physicians also found that diabeties is three times more prevalent among air traffic controllers than among second class airmen. "The onset of diabeties," stated the physicians, "is reported to be associated with periods of stress, particularly periods of grinding work and frustration without hope of relief."

Research is continuing, but the findings of Cobb and Rose, reported in the January 23, 1973, *Journal of The American Medical Association,* indicate there is more validity to controllers' reports of work-related physical and emotional costs of air traffic control than some FAA officials are willing to admit—or to deal with.

Controllers in Los Angeles often told me, and psychiatrists confirmed, that a major source of stress is the fear that in the event of a crash the FAA will do whatever it feels it can get away with to "hang" the controller with responsibility for the accident. The following incident is an example of how such fear develops.

At Los Angeles TRACON we had this private plane coming off of Long Beach going to Santa Monica, just north of LAX. Stadium sent him over Hollywood Park at 4,000, then descended him down to 3,000, paralleling the 32-degree [Los Angeles VOR] radial toward Santa Monica.

We were so busy working jets; we were IFR on parallel approaches —we were just turning and burning. Suddenly the Downey hand-off man turns to the Stadium radar controller and shouts, 'Get that guy outta there!' The Stadium controller called the pilot and issued him new instructions. The guy answered and that was the last we ever heard from him. We'd let the guy fly into a mountain.

We had an investigation right away and the TRACON deputy chief tried to get me to alter some documents to show that the Stadium hand-off position had been staffed at the time of the accident instead of empty. The deputy said, 'The log doesn't show the position was staffed and we'll have to show it as staffed.' I said, 'Don't give it a thought that you're going to get away with that shit!'

The deputy was trying to save his neck at the expense of the controller; and he was the kind of guy who was always coming around and saying, 'Don't worry about a thing; if you're right we'll back you all the way.'

After that accident the administration issued an order that the Stadium hand-off position would be staffed at all times. It's still not staffed a lot of time during the arrival rushes, but if there's another accident when it isn't staffed the administration can hang the arrival team supervisor and the A.C.

They'll just say, 'The air traffic control supervisors on duty did not follow prescribed procedures,' and that's it; the administration's off the hook.

Never mind that the shift might be short-handed, that maybe nobody got off their positions to eat, and that a lot of people there might be working overtime. What they should do is hire enough people.

Another controller—at Los Angeles tower—said it this way, "Regulations are broken every day at LAX to move the metal, to put it there on the runway and take it off, because there's no other way in hell to do it. The FAA says, 'Go by the book,' but if you ever went by the book traffic would be backed up all the way to hell.

"The management never comes up here to the tower; they don't want to know what goes on up here. They hang your ass if anything happens, but if we ever go by the book the FAA screams 'Slowdown.' You lay your neck on the chopping block every time you climb those stairs. The administration doesn't really give a shit about what happens to the controller. They don't care what the job does to us, all they want is for us not to have any deals because it's embarrassing for them. Everyone who works here has the feeling that, 'If I get into trouble, I'm on my own unless it's to the management's benefit to help me out; but if it's to their benefit to screw me, they'll screw me that fast!'

"You've got to have the feeling that somebody's standing there to back you up. Here they're standing there ready to put a knife in you if that will help them."

But there is another place to look for confirmation of controller stress: between the pages of a report detailing the findings of a committee commissioned by the Department of Transportation, mandated to take a careful look at air traffic controllers' working conditions and job demands.

Before listing its recommendations to the Department of Transportation and the FAA, the committee noted that an air traffic controller must have a highly developed capacity for spatial perception; a keenly developed, quick, and retentive memory; a capacity for articulate and decisive verbal communication; and a capacity for rapid decision making, combined with a mature judgment.

The introduction to the report stated that, upon the basis of exhaustive and wide-ranging study, the committee had determined:

There is compelling evidence that many controllers work for varying periods of time under great stress. They are confronted with the necessity of making successive life and death decisions within very short time-frames—decisions requiring constant standards of perfection.

The operations schedule in most facilities requires that the personnel work on a twenty-four-hour, multi-shift basis, 365 days a year. This schedule adds to the day-to-day wear and tear on the individual and to the disruption of normal family and social relationships. The controller is convinced that he will 'burn out' between ages forty and fifty and will not be able to continue controlling traffic.

During its interviews with approximately 400 controllers and 100 supervisors at about thirty facilities, the committee found:

1. clear cut evidence of a strong biochemical response by air traffic controller personnel . . . to conditions which were perceived within their bodies as acutely stressful;

2. a sharp increase of errors among older controllers;

3. a lack of adequate incentive to attract personnel to higher density facilities; and

4. a practice followed by the FAA of preventing the individual from transferring out of these [high-density] facilities once he has been assigned there because his services are urgently needed there.

In commenting upon the FAA's reluctance to permit controller transfers from high-density facilities, the Committee stated that

an especially demoralizing result of the lack of mobility [away from these facilities] is exemplified by the older controller who, having worked his way up to the rank of journeyman controller in one of the larger, critical facilities, reaches the point of 'burn out.'

His productive working life might be materially extended, to the advantage of the service, if he could be transferred to a facility handling a lesser volume of traffic, promoted to a supervisory assignment, or assigned other work within the FAA for which his experience is qualifying. At present, however, he is effectively denied the opportunity to transfer to an assignment at a smaller facility. . . .

Among its numerous suggestions the Committee recommended that the FAA:

1. provide monetary attraction for employment at certain high-density/high cost-of-living facilities by inaugurating special pay rates,

2. revise and make realistic the criteria under which facilities are rated and individuals are graded,

3. develop various incentives which will attract the most talented controllers to the most difficult assignments and provide a means to relieve them of these arduous duties after a reasonable period of time,

4. provide longer intervals between shift rotations (i.e., instead of weekly or less, rotate quarterly, semi-annually, or annually),

5. formulate a proposal for higher compensation within the journeyman grade and aggressively seek authority . . . to pay such compensation to controllers in high cost-of-living areas; and

6. place no restrictions on the freedom of controllers who have spent ten years or more in a high-density facility to transfer laterally (without loss of pay) to less demanding positions.

Although the findings of the Committee closely parallel the more individual findings of the psychiatrists quoted earlier, and, although the suggestions made by the Committee seem reasonable enough, not one of the recommendations listed has been implemented.

There has been time; the report, commonly called the "Corson Committee Report," was submitted to the Department of Transportation and the FAA—in 1970.

29 The Bureaucracy Factor

At the earliest possible date, air traffic control should be removed from the Federal Aviation Administration and transferred to a quasi-government corporation similar to AMTRAK, COMSAT, the Federal Reserve Bank, and similar government corporations. Under FAA management, air traffic services have become overly complex, increasingly inefficient, far too costly . . . and a hazard to public safety.

THE FEDERAL Aviation Administration, created in 1938 by the federal government as the Civil Aeronautics Authority, is, after several name changes and loss of status as an independent agency, a part of the Department of Transportation (DOT). The FAA Administrator, under the thumb of the DOT, has little room to function at the policy level and must clear minor administrative appointments, news releases, and even the time and length of coffee breaks with the Department of Transportation. Policy proposals, such as the Administrator's recommendation for the establishment of an FAA Office of Aviation Safety, often wait the better part of a year for word of DOT approval or disapproval.

231

The FAA's budget is $2.7 billion (for 1978), and growing. It is involved in multi-million dollar "safety" research programs which, even if technically feasible, have a potential cost-effectiveness about equal to a requirement that all automobile drivers and passengers wear crash helmets.

Some of these programs attempt to insure, through the use of highly-complicated and costly ground-based and airborne equipment, against the possibility of a mid-air collision between two light planes flying over the Kansas countryside. The manpower and money absorbed by these projects could better be spent in high priority areas, such as landing and approach accidents (55 percent of all airline accident fatalities) and weather-related accidents (83 percent of all aircraft accidents during the past fifteen years occurred under actual instrument conditions), than along current lines of collision research which, including airlines, accounts for no more than 4 percent of total aircraft accident fatalities and 2 percent of all aircraft accidents.

Recently established air traffic policies place under-qualified, and in many cases inept, controllers in a position to provide so-called air traffic separation services which are neither necessary nor desired by the vast majority of pilots. The FAA's policy in this area is comparable to requiring a clumsy intern to perform intricate brain surgery on an individual who doesn't need it.

The FAA operates slightly more than 500 airport control towers, 400 instrument landing systems, 21 en route air traffic control centers, and 160 radar approach control facilities. The FAA employs a lot of people for the job it does: 56,000 of the 75,000 total within the Department of Transportation. The National Aeronautics and Space Administration has 27,000 employees; the Atomic Energy Commission, about 8,000; and the entire Department of Commerce, only 36,000. The FAA's 56,000 employees equal one full-time employee for every 2.6 airplanes in the entire United States civil fleet. That's enough manpower to assign one FAA employee to every individual airplane for fifteen hours and twenty minutes every week—more time than the airplane is *flown*. Comparing the number of its employees to United

States certificated pilots, the FAA could assign one full-time employee to each individual pilot in the United States for two hours and forty-five minutes each week; far more time than a physician spends with each hospital patient he sees during any seven days.

Dividing the FAA's $2-billion budget into the number of United States civil aircraft reveals that the FAA spends more than $15,000 each year for each airplane registered in the United States. Seventy percent of the FAA's budget is paid for by user charges, aviation fuel taxes, etc., and 30 percent, somewhat lower than the proportion of federal highway support, comes from general revenues. Perhaps the FAA's $2.7-billion annual budget and one employee for every 2.6 airplanes in the United States might be justified if the FAA's "customers," airline and non-airline pilots, felt the agency was doing its job. But they do not. Even the FAA's front line troops who man its control towers and radar facilities have lost confidence in the Federal Aviation Administration's ability to operate a safe air traffic control system.

In July of 1974, after an exhaustive study of the air traffic system and its effect upon scheduled airline operations, six highly-experienced, recently-retired airline captains with a total of more than 160,000 flying hours submitted to the Federal Aviation Administration a detailed report outlining the results of their investigation, a project which had been commissioned by the FAA itself. After visiting a wide range of air traffic control facilities and observing cockpit procedures and workloads aboard some 600 airline flights operated by twenty-seven airlines, the captains found that

1. the numerous communications demands of air traffic control caused a serious deterioration of safety;

2. in accomplishing its task of traffic separation and flow, the FAA has created hazards, slowed traffic, restricted productive flight by all segments of the aviation industry and used energy in frightening amounts;

3. the system is a jumble of people, radarscopes, communications lines, and stacks of paper strips. . . . It is obvious that the system is reaching a point of 'critical mass.' Its methods, confu-

sion, and piling up of radar and people as traffic grows, will not suffice for the future. It detracts from efficient aircraft operation and creates hazards which lead to accidents other than collision; and

4. The FAA has failed to grasp the significance of fatigue because those who administer the regulations and those who ride in airplane cockpits during line checks do not experience the cumulative results of protracted crew schedule mismanagement.

Finally, the airline captains' report recommended that a study be conducted to determine whether the air traffic system would be operated more efficiently with advanced technology as an independent public company.

These are not the only findings which the Special Air Safety Advisory Group submitted to the FAA. Other recommendations listed the need for additional landing and approach aids, better controller understanding of cockpit workloads, and far better cockpit discipline by pilots themselves.

General aviation organizations, representing individual and corporate aircraft owners and operators who transport nearly 50 percent of airplane passengers, and who operate 98 percent of the United States civil aviation fleet and 72 percent of all civil aircraft hours flown, are also disappointed and concerned about the FAA's management of the air traffic system.

The Aircraft Owners and Pilots Association, National Business Aircraft Association, and National Pilots Association have repeatedly expressed concern about FAA "taxation without representation" manifested by increased costs for unnecessary "services" which delay aircraft, raise operating costs, and too often endanger pilots, passengers, and people on the ground.

Increasingly, aircraft operators, including those of scheduled airlines, are finding themselves required to operate their aircraft more in accordance with the needs of the air traffic system than to accomplish the purpose of the flight. Frequently, the system demands flight maneuvers and performance beyond the capability of the aircraft.

A study recently conducted by the Air Transport Association

(ATA), the association of United States scheduled airlines, revealed that, since the introduction of air traffic "automation" (computer-assisted hand-offs, flight strip printing, and radar data processing), air traffic delays have *increased,* despite the fact that operations have been reduced. The ATA estimates that air traffic system-inadequacies waste from 130 to 150 million gallons of fuel per year.

The National Transportation Safety Board (NTSB), an independent government agency which investigates and determines the probable cause of civil aircraft accidents, has repeatedly found its safety recommendations ignored, lost, and often even unacknowledged by the FAA.

In a March, 1975, report, the General Accounting Office stated that the "FAA's procedures permit promised actions to be dormant for extended periods or to be forgotten." In citing an example of delays in FAA follow-up on NTSB safety recommendations, the GAO report said:

After an accident in May, 1970, the NTSB recommended that the FAA eliminate, within a reasonable period, the use of fabric-to-metal seatbelt buckles and require metal-to-metal seatbelt buckles on United States registry aircraft. In its investigation [of an accident] the NTSB found that seven passengers had been thrown from their seats despite having their seatbelts fastened. In making its recommendations, the NTSB also cited other instances in which fabric-to-metal buckles had failed.

In October, 1970, the FAA said that it was studying this matter. In September, 1974, four years after the NTSB recommended action 'within a reasonable period,' the FAA was still studying fabric-to-metal seatbelt buckles.

The General Accounting Office study concluded that "the FAA often responds to a [safety] recommendation by making an internal directive or a public issuance. There is no follow-up, however, to determine if they are achieving their objectives and satisfying the [NTSB] recommendations."

The FAA is unaccountably slow in implementing its own

safety rules. During an NTSB investigation into the cause of a fatal corporate plane crash into a radio tower in Washington, D.C., during April of 1975, the FAA admitted that twenty days had elapsed between the time it issued an order requiring controllers to inform pilots of the appropriate altitude during various stages of approach and the time controllers began compliance with the order. During the interim, the corporate plane, flying 750 feet too low, crashed into the radio tower killing all five people aboard.

Often the FAA's response to a crash is to issue an order and to revise the air traffic control rulebook, mounting yet another responsibility upon the shoulders of already overburdened air traffic controllers rather than taking serious steps to solve the problem. In their report to the FAA, the six airline captains of the Special Air Safety Advisory Group stated that, "Partial solutions or the temporary imposing of additional procedures or mechanical stop-gap measures seriously complicate the smooth, safe functioning of the air transportation system. The trend toward partial solutions, which are expedient, must be reversed."

In perhaps the most thorough investigation of certain FAA expenditures ever conducted, the General Accounting Office (GAO), in a December, 1974, report, stated that the FAA spends unnecessary amounts of money on control towers, en route radio navigational facilities, and small airport lighting systems. In one comparison, between a non-FAA airport control tower at Jefferson City, Missouri, and an FAA-operated control tower at Norwood, Massachusetts—each tower with two control positions and operated sixteen hours per day—the GAO found that the cost of the FAA tower, $189,220, exceeded the cost of the non-FAA tower by $157,130. Equipment costs (1973) for the FAA tower were $31,400 compared to $7,240 for the non-FAA tower. Although the FAA tower cab is more spacious, controllers working in the Jefferson City tower said that the cab provided sufficient working space for controlling both air and ground traffic. The Jefferson City tower had two altimeters, as does the FAA tower, but had only one wind speed and direction indicator (FAA towers have two), one accurate clock (FAA towers have three), and one signal light gun, used in the event of aircraft or tower radio failure (FAA towers have two).

The GAO report found that, "FAA air traffic control towers for low-activity airports are more costly than those constructed by local governments. Although differences exist between FAA towers and non-FAA towers, both apparently perform the same functions satisfactorily. Under these circumstances it would appear that the FAA could save money by evaluating its low-activity tower requirements." The GAO also criticized the FAA for unnecessary spending to assure the 100 percent availability of certain en route navigational aids without determining the need. "The design and maintenance of FAA omnirange facilities result in more than 99 percent availability. Although such availability may be justified by safety considerations," said the GAO, "in some cases the associated cost is significant. . . . The FAA has not adequately considered the need for this degree of availability. . . ." FAA airport lighting costs for small airports are so high, according to the GAO, that many communities install lighting at their own expense rather than seek federal assistance.

The most recent and far-reaching study of the FAA's operation of the air traffic system, commissioned by the Professional Air Traffic Controllers Organization (PATCO) and conducted by the respected aviation consulting firm of Glen A. Gilbert & Associates, recommended that the air traffic function of the FAA be made the responsibility of a quasi-government corporation such as AMTRAK. The 1975 Glen A. Gilbert & Associates' report noted that the present air traffic system is forced to meet increasing demands with both hands tied behind its back. The FAA, the study points out, is 'under the thumb of the DOT.' FAA policy decisions are screened by DOT personnel who are unqualified in aviation matters and who have no responsibility for results. Under DOT rule, FAA plans affecting air traffic system users, who pay a good part of the bill, are interferred with by DOT—which does not provide for the participation of aviation groups, such as airlines and corporate and private aviation, in the decision-making process.

FAA cost-cutting and procurement efforts are hampered by a time-consuming DOT review process—to the extent that many companies, who may have innovative and inexpensive equipment and systems to offer, are no longer interested in doing business with the FAA/DOT. Under DOT, the FAA is not permitted to negotiate significantly on labor-management relations with FAA employees, and the FAA has no decision-making power to determine how, and to what extent, airport and airway user taxes are to be spent.

Internal morale, initiative, and innovative thinking have tended to deteriorate throughout the FAA.

Prior to the 1967 placement of the FAA under the DOT "umbrella," the nation's two most respected pilot organizations expressed serious concern. The Air Line Pilots Association (ALPA) suggested during a Senate hearing that the FAA remain an independent agency outside the DOT. The Aircraft Owners and Pilots Association (AOPA) also urged Congress to keep the FAA out of the Department of Transportation.

In making its recommendation that the air traffic system of the United States be operated by an AMTRAK-type government corporation, the Glen Gilbert report pointed out that, although direct user charges provide half of the entire FAA budget, users have no say at all in how the system is operated or funded and that the FAA is not responsive to the requirements of airspace users. Return of the FAA to its pre-1967 status as an independent agency would do much to alleviate delays and misunderstandings brought about by the Department of Transportation's failure to recognize aviation's importance to the nation's economic and social progress and its potential for reducing fuel consumption. (A 150-mile-an-hour, single-engine plane is far more fuel-efficient than the average auto—and, of course, travels fewer miles to get from one town to another.)

But past experience indicates that, even as an independent agency, the FAA cannot provide the economic and safe operation of the air traffic system which we require. The situation isn't going to get better. FAA forecasts indicate that within twelve years the demand for air traffic services will nearly double. Yet during that time there will not be a doubling of major hub airports; there will not be a doubling of runways at those airports; and there will not be a doubling of the major cities between which the majority of air traffic will travel. It is, in the words of one high-ranking official, "a frightening prospect."

The quasi-government United States Air Traffic Services Corporation proposed by the Glen A. Gilbert & Associates' study funded by PATCO, an organization of the FAA's own air traffic controllers, would be governed by a nine-person board of directors appointed by the President and confirmed by the Senate. The board would bring to the United States Air Traffic Services Corporation individuals with background and expertise from scheduled airline operations, non-scheduled airlines, military aviation, airline passengers, business aviation, personal aviation, and airport planning and management.

The establishment of the United States Air Traffic Services Corporation, recommended by Glen A. Gilbert & Associates and the Professional Air Traffic Controllers Organization—and suggested for consideration by the airline captains' Special Air Safety Advisory Group—is not the only answer, but it would be the first step toward the efficient management of today's air traffic system and the development of tomorrow's.

Epilogue

$\mathbb{E}$ ight months after leaving Los Angeles I was back at LAX tower and TRACON, this time to ask several of the controllers I knew best to read this book's completed manuscript for accuracy.

When I mounted the flight of stairs leading from the tower's ready-room to the cab, the local two position's "brite" radarscope had been pulled forward from the corner of the cab on its ceiling track so that it was almost in the center of the room.

Without speaking to anyone, I stood for a moment at the top of the stairs to pick up on the early afternoon activity, matching

what I heard with the movements of planes on LAX's four runways and taxiways below.

The controller closest to me was using a long pointer, touching
symbols on the radarscope as he asked the man beside him a series
of questions:

"And this, here, what's this?"

"Santa Monica?"

"How 'bout this one up here; what's this one?"

"I think that's Coliseum."

"And this, here; what's this?" Ted Merril asked, as he continued to quiz the new man.

When you're the oldest controller in the facility, like I am, you feel the other guys watching you—like they used to watch an aging gun-slinger, waiting for him to get slow. Every time you go to work you ask yourself, 'Is today gonna be it?', and you wonder, like in that song by Willie Nelson, 'Where has a slow-movin', once quick-draw outlaw got to go?'

—Los Angeles Air Traffic Controller